Georgetown Elementary School
Indian Prairie School District
Aurora, Illinois

TITLE I MATERIALS

First Place
Science Fair Projects
for Inquisitive Kids

First Place
Science Fair Projects
for Inquisitive Kids

Elizabeth Snoke Harris

LARK BOOKS
A Division of Sterling Publishing Co., Inc.
New York

Editor:
Rain Newcomb

Art Director:
Thom Gaines

Creative Director and Cover Designer:
Celia Naranjo

Production Assistance:
Jeff Hamilton
and Shannon Yokeley

Editorial Assistance:
Veronika Alice Gunter, Delores Gosnell,
and Nathalie Mornu

Photographer:
Steve Mann

Illustrator:
Orrin Lundgren

Proofreader:
Karen Levy

Library of Congress Cataloging-in-Publication Data

Harris, Elizabeth Snoke, 1973-
  First place science fair projects for inquisitive kids / Elizabeth Snoke
Harris.— 1st ed.
     p. cm.
  Includes index.
  ISBN 1-57990-493-9 (hardcover)
  1. Science projects. 2. Science—Experiments. I. Title.
Q182.3.H37 2005
507'.8—dc22

                                    2005013161

10 9 8 7 6 5 4 3 2 1

First Edition

Published by Lark Books, A Division of
Sterling Publishing Co., Inc.
387 Park Avenue South, New York, N.Y. 10016

Text © 2005, Elizabeth Snoke Harris
Photography and illustrations © 2005, Lark Books

Distributed in Canada by Sterling Publishing,
c/o Canadian Manda Group, 165 Dufferin Street
Toronto, Ontario, Canada M6K 3H6

Distributed in the U.K. by Guild of Master Craftsman Publications Ltd.,
Castle Place, 166 High Street, Lewes, East Sussex, England BN7 1XU
Tel: (+ 44) 1273 477374, Fax: (+ 44) 1273 478606,
e-mail: pubs@thegmcgroup.com, Web: www.gmcpublications.com

Distributed in Australia by Capricorn Link (Australia) Pty Ltd.,
P.O. Box 704, Windsor, NSW 2756 Australia

If you have questions or comments about this book, please contact:
Lark Books
67 Broadway
Asheville, NC 28801
(828) 253-0467

Manufactured in China

ISBN 1-57990-493-9

For information about custom editions, special sales, premium and
corporate purchases, please contact Sterling Special Sales Department
at 800-805-5489 or specialsales@sterlingpub.com.

Contents

Introduction

You're standing in the school gymnasium with all your classmates. It's time once again for the science fair. Except this year you totally forgot about it, and you're standing in front of a blank display. There's Suzie hauling in her experiment on rocket propulsion fuel. It looks like this time she outdid herself and actually made a rocket. Here comes Johnny with his experiment on oil sludge and drinking water. (It's not pretty.) You frantically search your pockets for a magic marker. Surely there's something you can write on your display!

Suddenly the judges are in front of your table, looking curiously at the gleaming white display board. "This is my science fair project on the effectiveness of invisible ink," you stammer. "Oh, you can't see anything? Well of course you can't! That's because my experiment worked so well!" You smile weakly while the judges give you that look.

Brrrrrriiiinnnnnnggggg!!!
Brrrrrriiiinnnnnnggggg!!!

You wake with a start. It was all just a bad dream! The science fair is still eight weeks away. You've got plenty of time to do your project. But to keep your nightmares at bay (because next time you might be in your underwear), you should start right now. That's where this book comes in. The answers to all your science fair questions are right here.

Making a great science fair project is a lot easier than you think. There's only one thing you need: Your curiosity about the world around you. (Here's what you don't need: a lab coat, goggles, a secret formula to make you a genius overnight, a storeroom full of beakers, a library full of 400-pound textbooks, or parents who'll do all the work for you.)

This book starts with a chapter on everything you need to know—from choosing a topic that intrigues you and making a schedule for exploring it, to designing your experiment and following it through to its successful conclusion. You'll find information on checking for errors in your experiment, doing the math, analyzing the data, and turning it all into impressive charts and graphs. And there's more. We've included 50 fantastic experiments that you can use for your science fair project: biology projects, physical science projects, and chemistry projects. Each project is set up so that you can use it without having to worry about cheating on your homework, because you have to do the work and figure out the results. There are also suggestions for designing your own experiments.

So, are you ready to sleep peacefully? Turn the page to get started on your science fair project.

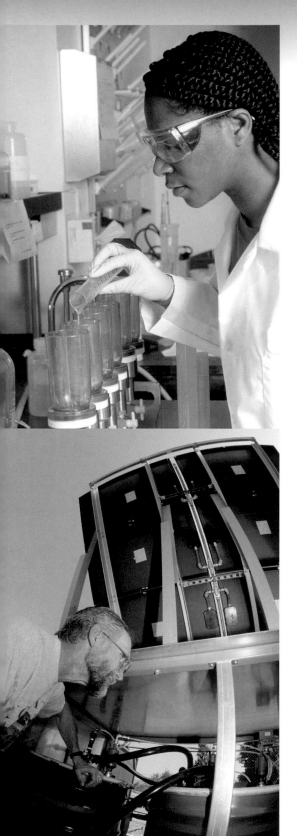

Science Fair Basics

In this section you'll find everything you need to know about science fair projects. From picking a topic and forming a hypothesis to designing your experiment and making a display, it's all right here. Your experiment will be a success—it may even win you a prize! And you'll have fun being a scientist.

Discovering Your Inner Scientist

Have you ever met a real live scientist before? If not, find the nearest mirror and take a look. You've been a scientist since the day you were born.

Science is just a way of exploring the world around you. When you took your first steps, you investigated the physics of balance and equilibrium. The last time you played basketball, you explored projectile motion, changing the speed and direction of the ball to get it through the hoop. Each attempt to convince your mother that you've already cleaned your room is actually a study in human behavior. Even washing the dishes is an investigation into the chemistry of surfactants (that means soap). You might not be wearing a lab coat, taking measurements, and formally analyzing data, but you're still a scientist!

Secrets of Success

So what is the secret to a fabulous science fair project, anyway? Well, there are three of them:

1 **Come up with a fun, original question that you are really excited about.**

You've probably got lots of these stuck in your head. The steps on pages 12 and 13 will help you get them out of your head and into your Science Fair Project Notebook.

2 **Follow the scientific method to find an answer to your question.**

The scientific method is a set of guidelines that scientists like you use to answer their fascinating questions (see Secret #1). Don't sweat the details right now. I'll walk you through each step in the section on pages 14 to 18.

3 **Do the best work you can do.**

This is the most important part of your science fair project. It isn't hard and requires no special equipment. Just work as carefully and as methodically as you can. Your best will come out!

Plan of Action

Your science fair project is simply another way to explore the world around you—only this time with a plan. Just as no evil genius would set out to conquer the world without a master plan, a good scientist wouldn't start an experiment without a well-thought out plan. A good plan of action will cut down on the time it takes to do your experiment, ensure more accurate results, and allow another scientist to duplicate your experiment to verify your results. This section will tell you everything you need to know to come up with a foolproof plan for your project.

Get a Notebook

This is the absolute very first thing you need to do. This will be your lab notebook, and it will ONLY be used for your science fair project. Any type of notebook will do as long as it has paper and a cover to keep things such as water, chemicals, and your little sister from getting inside. Put your name on it, and if you like, write some intimidating warning to keep other people out. Anytime you do anything related to your project (and this includes middle-of-the-night "what if…" thoughts), write it down in your notebook. Be sure to keep your lab notebook handy.

Make a Schedule

Hopefully, you're not reading this book the night before the fair and you've given yourself some time to do your project. Find out when the fair is and mark it on a calendar. Figure out how much time you have to work on your project and make a schedule. Ideally, you should have about eight weeks to do your project. This might sound like a long time, but remember Secret #3? (Turn to page 9 if you've already forgotten.) Figure out whether your project is going to require anything such as growing plants, collecting dandelion seedpods, or other time-sensitive things. Take this into account! Try to finish your experiment a week or two before the fair so you have time to write your report and make your display. Most important, make sure the schedule is realistic and you can actually stick to it.

While you're at it, it wouldn't hurt to get a copy of the rules to make sure you know what you're supposed to do. Some science fairs only let you do biology projects or won't let you do anything using animals. Figure this out now rather than after you've done six or eight weeks of work.

Checklist for Success #1:

Eight-Week Schedule Checklist

If you have eight weeks before the science fair, you can use this schedule as is. Check off each task as you complete it. Go ahead—it feels good—and it gives you a sense of real accomplishment. Write the dates in the spaces provided, and get to work. If you have more than eight weeks, don't wait. Simply give yourself more time to do some of the tasks. Or, get started and finish early. Hey, why not!?

Week #1 (dates: _____)

☐ Choose your topic.
☐ Organize your notebook.
☐ Ask questions.

Week #2 (dates: _____)

☐ Research your chosen topic.

Week #3 (dates: _____)

☐ Finish your research.
☐ Define your problem.
☐ Develop your hypothesis.
☐ Design your experiment.

Week #4 (dates: _____)

☐ Turn in an experiment summary to your teacher.
☐ Gather all needed materials for your experiment.
☐ Start your experiment.

Week #5 (dates: _____)

☐ Set up an outline for your project report.
☐ Continue your experiment.
☐ Begin collecting materials for your display.

Week #6 (dates: _____)

☐ Continue your experiment.
☐ Write the first draft of your project report.
☐ Sketch some designs for your display.

Week #7 (dates: _____)

☐ Finish your experiment.
☐ Revise list of materials needed for the experiment and the steps of the procedure, if necessary.
☐ Analyze your data, and draw your conclusions.
☐ Revise the project report.

Week #8 (dates: _____)

☐ Complete your display.
☐ Edit and type the final draft of the project report.
☐ Prepare for the fair.

The Fair (date: _____)

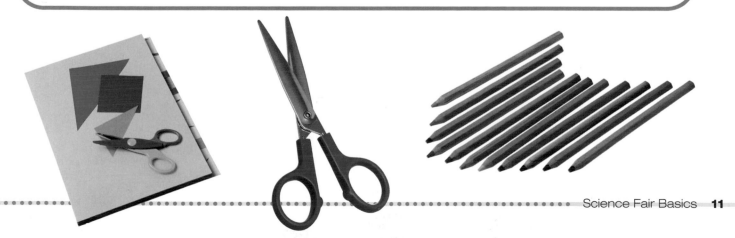

Pick a Topic

Since you'll be working on your project for at least two months, the topic should be something you really like. Picking a topic is much less intimidating than it seems. All you really need to do to pick a topic is think and write. (You might think you already know exactly what you want to do, but it never hurts to have a couple of backup ideas in case something doesn't work out.)

First, think of things you like to do. What are your hobbies? What are you interested in? What do you enjoy doing? Open up your lab notebook and write these things down on the first page. It doesn't matter how silly or crazy they sound; you're just getting a starting point.

If you're still having trouble, look around and pay attention to what you do every day. Look through the newspaper and talk to your friends and family. You've got lots of great resources right in front of you. Make a list of these things in your lab notebook.

Now that you have a list of potential topics, it's time to narrow it down a little. If you wrote down "sports," write down a particular sport you like. If you wrote down "being out-doors," write down what you like

about being outdoors. Is it the plants, trees, water, dirt, or bugs? If you wrote down "food," cross it out and write down some specific foods that you like.

Take another look at the list. Pick one of the topics you have written down to be the basis for your project. (This is the hard part.) Keep the list around, though, since the odds are you'll be doing another science fair project next year, and it might come in handy.

Congratulations! You have a topic.

Research Time

Now you're ready to research your topic. Write down everything you already know about the topic in your lab notebook. What do you like best about it? Go to the library and check out some books. (Then actually read them.) Find some experts on the topic and talk to them. Your friends and family might have information to share as well. Make sure you write down in your lab notebook what sources you're looking at (books, magazines, etc.), who you talk to, and all the interesting facts you come across.

Once you know a little more about your topic, you can start thinking up questions.

Choose a Question

Obviously, you need to have some questions before you can pick just one. Pull out that handy lab notebook again and write down every question you can think of about the topic you chose. Right now you just need a bunch of questions. It doesn't matter whether they're good, bad, or really easy to answer. I'll help you fix that later. If you get stuck trying to think up questions, look back at the notes you took from your research. It doesn't really matter how many questions you think of, but three is a good number to aim for. Make sure the questions can't be answered with a simple yes or no.

For example, suppose you chose popcorn, your favorite food, as your topic. Some questions could be:

What makes popcorn pop?

How is microwave popcorn different from air-popped popcorn?

Does it matter whether you butter the popcorn before or after you pop it?

How can I get the most popcorn without burning it in the microwave?

Now look at your list of questions and ask yourself, "Can I measure something to help answer one of these questions?"

Looking at the list of popcorn questions, only the last one has something you can easily measure: the amount of popcorn. This question looks promising, so you can explore it further.

> **Checklist for Success #2:**
> ## Choosing a Good Topic
>
> ✔ I'm interested in my topic and am looking forward to learning more about it.
>
> My question can be answered by taking measurements from an experiment.
>
> My question is open-ended. It can be answered with more than a yes or no.
>
> I can do most of the work myself in the time I have.
>
> My topic follows all rules and guidelines and won't blow up the kitchen.
>
> I have teacher approval.
>
> I can get all the materials needed for the experiment. (I don't need radioactive space debris or an electron microscope.)

> **Good science questions usually come in a specific form. For instance:**
>
> *How does _____ affect _____?*
>
> *How does _____ compare to _____?*
>
> *How does _____ determine _____?*
>
> You just need to fill in the blanks.

So let's look at our popcorn question again to see whether we can put it in the question formats to the left.

How does <u>the amount of time in the microwave</u> affect <u>the number of burnt kernels</u>?

I think we have a winner!

If you can't make one of your questions into a project, scratch it and pick another question. (That's why you wrote down more than one.)

The key to making the scientific method work for you:

It's simple. Take good notes in your lab notebook. Write down what you do, how you do it, and what you see. What seems like a silly observation at the time might be very important later. Draw lots of pictures, too. (It doesn't matter if you can't draw. You aren't being judged on your artistic ability. Label different parts of the sketch to make it clear what you've drawn.)

Get Started with the Scientific Method

The scientific method is a set of guidelines that scientists use to help them answer questions. It's pretty straightforward, and you've already done the first two steps: researched and identified a problem. Now you just need to form a hypothesis, design an experiment, perform the experiment, and analyze the results.

Form a Hypothesis

The first step is to make a *hypothesis*. A hypothesis is just a guess at the answer to your question. All you need to do is take your question and make it into an answer.

Examples

I think _____ will affect _____.

    OR I think _____ will not affect _____.

I believe_____ will determine _____.

    OR I believe _____ will not determine _____.

Don't stress out about whether your guess is right or wrong. At this stage, it doesn't matter. You haven't done your experiment, so you aren't supposed to know the answer—yet. Besides, you might learn more if what actually happens is not what you expected. It's okay if your final results don't support your hypothesis. The science fair judges won't count off for this. (Just make sure you can explain to them why you chose the hypothesis you did!)

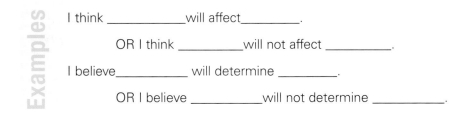

Using our popcorn example, one hypothesis might be:

I think *the amount of time the popcorn cooks in the microwave* will determine *the number of burnt popcorn kernels.*

See how easy that was? I chose this hypothesis from my past experiences of leaving the popcorn in the microwave for too long and getting a smelly black mess.

Design Your Experiment

At this point you might think you're ready to jump in and start working on your experiment, but you're wrong. It'll save a lot of time later if you make a game plan first. You guessed it—pull out that lab notebook and start scribbling. There are three basic parts to your experiment.

1 The Independent Variable

The *independent variable* is what you change in the experiment. You're in charge of how it changes, and it doesn't depend on anything else. This is usually the same thing as the first blank of your question from page 14. In our case, that would be the amount of time the popcorn is in the microwave. Make sure you only have ONE independent variable. If you're testing more than one thing at a time, it'll be very difficult to draw an accurate conclusion.

Now that you know what you're going to change, you need to decide how you're going to change it. What time will you start with? How much should you increase it? How high should you go? You might need to refer to your research to make these decisions.

 Most bags of microwave popcorn give the optimal popping time—usually 1 to 4 minutes. Start with 1 minute and increase the time by 1 minute each time until you've increased the time to 4 minutes. This will give you four different cooking times. You can always go

back and change this if it doesn't give you enough information to answer the question.

Also think about how many trials you're going to run at each popping time. That is, how many bags of popcorn are you going to pop? Doing more trials helps get rid of *random error* (see page 16 for more information on random error). Three trials are acceptable, but more is better. That means for each of the four popping times you should pop three bags of popcorn at that time. So, if you have four different times and you're running three trials at each time, you'll be popping 12 bags of popcorn. That's a lot of popcorn! You might have to throw a popcorn party when you're done with this experiment.

2 The Dependent Variable

Decide what you're going to measure and how you're going to measure it. What you're going to measure is also known as the *dependent variable*. It's called that because it depends on what happens to your independent variable. In other words, when you change your independent variable, your dependent variable will change too. This is the same thing that is in the second blank of your question on page 14 (gee, that sure is coming in handy!).

 In our case, that would be the number of burnt popcorn kernels in each bag. You can measure this just by counting them. Of course, you need to decide how

much of a kernel needs to be burnt in order to count it. Measuring your dependent variable might not always be so simple. You may need to design an *apparatus*, which is an unusual piece of equipment or tool, or use an instrument such as a thermometer, ruler, or stopwatch to take the measurement.

3 The Controls

Finally, you need to decide what other variables you're going to control. That is, what other factors might affect the number of burnt kernels besides the time in the microwave? Make sure that these don't change during the experiment. These things are your controls.

 Some variables to control might be the brand of popcorn, whether it's buttered or unbuttered, the age of the popcorn, the temperature of the microwave, the type of microwave, and the power setting on the microwave. That's a lot of stuff to keep track of. Write it all down in your lab notebook. (That'll keep you from forgetting anything AND impress the judges!)

Error X

Let's face it, no scientist is perfect, not even you. This means every experiment is going to have some sort of error. The key to dealing with error is to jump the gun and point it out before other folks (like the judges) can call you on it.

Error can affect how *accurate* and *precise* your measurements are. While these two words are used together a lot, they actually mean very different things.

Precision just means that the measurements are always close together and accuracy means that the measurements are close to the true or real value.

You can be precise and not accurate or accurate and not precise. Your goal is to be both!

There are two types of error that will affect the accuracy and precision of your data.

Systematic error is caused when you do the same thing wrong every time. Most of the time you don't even know it, because hopefully if you did you would stop doing it! Systematic error usually causes problems with accuracy.

Random error is when factors, usually out of your control, affect your measurement differently each time. Sometimes you might measure low and other times high. You can still get an accurate reading but it won't be very precise.

Your job is to get rid of systematic and random error so that your measurements are precise and accurate! When writing your report and talking to judges it is important to be as specific as possible about where error might have popped up in your experiment. Here are some things to look for:

Mistakes
Of course these are going to cause errors! You can prevent these by working slowly and carefully. Don't be afraid to redo a measurement if you think you made a mistake.

Human error
This gets confused with mistakes a lot because humans are usually the ones making mistakes. However, human error has to do with the fact that we don't have perfect vision and steady hands all the time. Human error can also occur if you haven't had a lot of practice using a measuring instrument.

Instrument error
Most of your measuring devices have a bit of error built into them. If your ruler only has marks every millimeter, then the smallest you can measure, no matter how hard you try, is 0.5 millimeters. You may also want to take a close look at your ruler while you're at it and make sure the end is really 0 millimeters. Sometimes rulers (and other instruments) get worn or are printed wrong so the end is not exactly 0.

Observing the system
Taking a measurement can change what you're measuring! When you place a thermometer in a container of hot liquid, the cool thermometer might actually lower the temperature of the liquid while you measure its temperature. Also be careful when you're working with people since they might behave differently when they know they are being studied.

Sampling
The more data you collect, the less likely you're to have random error. If you only take one measurement there is no way to know if it is accurate or not. If you average lots of values (at least three but more is better) then you have a better chance of having an accurate value.

Science Fair Safety

When in doubt, ask for help. If you're not sure that you can handle a part of the experiment by yourself, it is all right to get an adult helper. This is especially true when you're dealing with candles, household chemicals, or the stove. Some experiments in this book will require an adult helper.

Wear goggles if you're using liquids, fire, or anything that can fly through the air. This is particularly important if you wear contact lenses because acids can actually melt your contact lens onto your eyeball!

Always wear closed-toe shoes like sneakers or shoes that tie. You don't want to drop anything heavy or spill anything dangerous onto your feet.

Read the labels on household chemicals for safety warnings and important protective measures such as wearing gloves.

No eating or drinking in the lab. Even if you're in the kitchen, you should not eat while doing science since the food can contaminate the experiment and the experiment can contaminate you!

Clean up before and after your experiment. Be sure your workspace is clean before you start and don't leave a mess when you're done.

Keep the TV and radio off. Loud music and TV shows can be distracting. To do good science and prevent dangerous mistakes, you want to be sure you can focus while you work.

Do Your Experiment

This is the part you've been waiting for! Gather your materials together, call up a couple of helpers if you need them, and get to it. Just remember to work slowly and carefully, and be aware of what you're doing. A sloppy experiment is not the way to science fair fame.

Use your lab notebook while you're working. Write down your measurements neatly so you don't have to redo the experiment later. Be sure to note any adjustments you make to your design and any observations that you didn't expect. Take pictures and draw diagrams. But most of all, have fun!

Do the Math

Now that you've done your experiment, you've got a bunch of numbers—*data*, if you want to be scientific about it. You need to turn those numbers into something you can use to answer your question.

Average your trials for each popping time. Calculate the percentage of popped and unpopped kernels or burnt and unburnt kernels. (For more information on doing the math, see page 57.) You can even visualize your data using a graph. (See pages 21 and 22 for help with this). This will make the next step much easier.

Analyze Your Data

At this point you've got some results, but what does it all mean? Do you see any patterns? How did the dependent variable (burnt popcorn kernels) change as you varied the independent variable (time in the microwave)? Are there any *outliers*, which are really weird data points that don't fit in with the rest of your measurements? You might consider throwing these away or retaking that measurement.

If you're having trouble at this step, you might want to consider retaking some measurements or trying something a little different with your procedure. It's okay to go back and adjust the way you take a measurement or set up the equipment. Just write it down in your lab notebook! Repeat each of your trials with the new setup.

Draw a Conclusion

Now it's time to answer your question. What does the data tell you? Is your hypothesis supported or not? A hypothesis is never right or wrong. Someone could design another experiment that contradicts your hypothesis even if your experiment supports it, and you could both be right. Science is usually more complex than right and wrong answers. Generally, the process you took to reach your conclusion is just as important as the conclusion itself.

If you can't answer your question from the data, don't freak out! Don't try to force an answer out of nothing. Can you collect more data or do another experiment to find the answer? The science fair judges won't mind if you can't find an answer as long as your experiment is done well and you have a plan for further experiments. (Mmmm, sounds like a project for next year!)

Prepare for the Fair

Congratulations! You've answered your science fair question and learned something. Now it's time to share your findings with the rest of the world. Most science fairs require a written report and a display. Here are some tips to make doing both of these things easy.

Write Your Report

This is simple—just look in your lab notebook! All of these sections are probably already written down in there somewhere; it's just a matter of finding the information.

Title Page

This should be short and to the point. Your title shouldn't be longer than your report. A good place to look for title ideas is in your research questions. Also, be sure to include your name, grade, the date, and your school on the title page.

Abstract

The purpose of the abstract is to give people an idea of what your project is about so they can decide whether they want to read the entire report. All you need is a couple of sentences that say what your project is about and what you found out.

Introduction

The introduction is where you explain what your project is all about. What question are you trying to answer? How did you choose this topic? Why is this an important subject to study? You might also want to include important background information you found in your research.

How Did You Do Your Experiment?

Think of this section as a story about how you did your experiment rather than instructions for doing it again. Describe what you did, what you measured, and what materials you used. What were your dependent and independent variables?

What were your controls and how did you control them? Include any problems you ran into and how you dealt with them. This is also a good place to put a drawing or photo of your setup. Be sure to label all the parts.

Data

This is where you put your graphs and data tables. However, if you made a graph of your data, you don't need a table with the same data. (See pages 21 and 22 for more information about charts and graphs.) Make sure you have the appropriate labels. Don't forget the units of measurement.

Discuss Your Data

What do your graphs and tables show? Point out any patterns or trends you want the reader (or the judges) to notice.

Conclusion

Here's your chance to explain what it all means and give the answer to your question. Is there anything you would do differently? Did you come up with more questions than answers? What are some ideas for further research?

Put Together Your Display

For the actual science fair you'll need a display. This is usually a three-paneled, freestanding board that you can buy at most office and school supply stores. Be sure to check your science fair rules for restrictions on space and size for your display so you don't get disqualified! Here are some tips for making a super display:

▶ Less Is More

Don't make your board too wordy. You need to leave something to talk about with the judges. Use lists instead of paragraphs where possible (such as your procedure and conclusions). The judges don't have an hour to spend reading all the parts of your board.

▶ Use Pictures

If you can use pictures instead of words to show your procedure and setup clearly, then do it! However, don't include extra, unrelated pictures just for decoration. Every picture should be up there for a reason. Be sure to label the important parts of a picture or diagram that you want the judges to notice.

▶ Keep It Simple

Make sure your board isn't crowded. Empty space is a good thing. Also pay attention to the colors you choose. Don't put pink words on a blue background or do anything that will make the judges cross-eyed.

▶ Keep It Neat

Use a computer, word processor, or stencils to print out all the parts of your display so you don't have to worry about handwriting. Use rubber cement to attach paper to your board. (Glue can make the paper look crumpled.) Don't use staples; most boards aren't thick enough to hold them.

▶ Check the Rules!

If you plan on including your apparatus, instruments, or other items with your display, check to make sure the rules allow this. Animals, in particular, even fish and insects, are usually restricted.

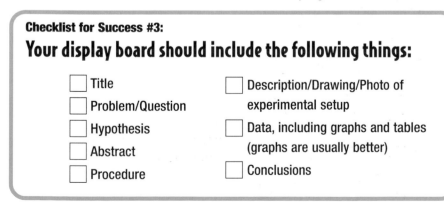

Before You Go to the Fair

There isn't a whole lot you can do right now to improve your project, but being prepared for the fair will help you have a good time.

▶ Double-check the rules one more time for what you're allowed to bring. Check the date, time, and place while you're at it.

▶ Practice. Have your parents or friends pretend to be judges, and practice talking about your project. If you can explain your experiment to your grandmother, then you can explain it to anyone!

▶ Gather everything together that you're going to bring to the fair such as your display, notebook, and any approved apparatus from your project that you might like to show the judges.

▶ Dress nicely. Don't wear a hat or sloppy clothes. It can't hurt to make a good impression.

While You're There

You've done everything you can, so now just enjoy the fair. Each fair is different. You might need to stand by your project the whole time and talk to all sorts of people, such as parents and teachers, about the project. You might not even know which ones are the judges! At some fairs, the judges just look at the displays and don't even talk to the scientists. It's always better to get a chance to talk to the judges so they can see how important your project is to you.

You can use the report you wrote to help make your presentation. But don't read your report! Talk to the people who come up to your display. Start with your abstract, then walk them through your hypothesis, procedure, data, and conclusions, then summarize what you just said in a couple of sentences. Mention any interesting questions that came up during your experiment. What would you like to investigate next on this problem?

Tips for Talking to the Judges

▶ Talk slowly and clearly.

▶ Don't read off your display.

▶ Explain what everything is and how it relates to your experiment.

▶ Remember that the judges are on your side. They want to see how well you have done.

▶ Relax and smile!

Above all, be honest. Don't try to cover up the errors you made. Explain what they were and how you would do things differently if you had more time. If you don't know the answer to a question, that's okay! It's better to admit you don't know then to try to make something up. (The judges will know.) Offer to look up the answer and send it to them later. Be proud of the good work you have done.

Charts, Graphs & Tables

Charts and graphs are a great way to present your data, not just because they look great on a display board but also because they organize your data in ways that can be understood easily and quickly. There are many different ways to create graphs and tables and some are better than others depending on the type of data you have. Here are the four most common examples.

Data Tables

You've collected lots of numbers and you want to show them all off. A data table seems like the best way to do this. Think again. Data tables should be used sparingly. Although they are perfect for collecting your data, when preparing for your display board, a big table of numbers can seem overwhelming and confusing. However, if you have four or less numbers, a data table isn't such a bad idea.

When you put your table together, be sure to label each column of data and include the units of measurement. Don't forget a title too. The left-hand column should contain your independent variable, while the columns to the right contain you dependent variables.

Bar Graph

When your data is *nominal*, that is, your independent variables are names or things rather than amounts, a bar graph is the way to go. For example you can use a bar graph to look at average number of popped kernels in different types of popcorn or to compare how different classes did on a social studies test. Bar graphs are used mostly to compare a set of measurements. The horizontal axis should always contain the independent variable and the vertical axis shows the dependent variable or what you measured. Be sure to label the axes and don't forget the units of measurement too.

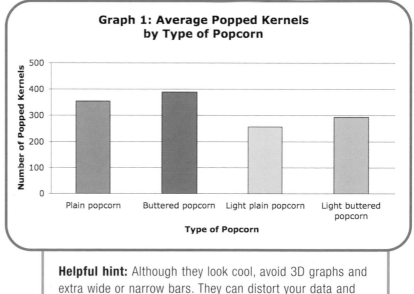

Helpful hint: Although they look cool, avoid 3D graphs and extra wide or narrow bars. They can distort your data and make it difficult to compare values.

Line Graph

A line graph is perfect if your data is *ordinal*. This means your independent variable is a number or an amount such as time in the microwave. Line graphs are used to show patterns or changes over time. Just like with a bar graph, the horizontal axis should always contain the independent variable and the vertical axis shows the dependent variable or what you measured. Be sure to label the axes and don't forget the units of measurement too. If you have multiple sets of data sets on the same graph, use different colors or symbols for the different sets of data.

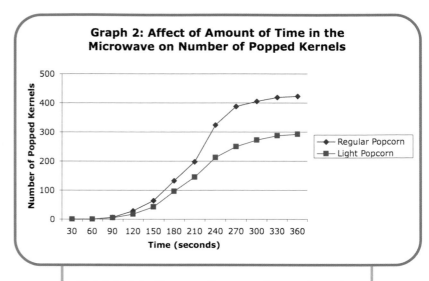

Graph 2: Affect of Amount of Time in the Microwave on Number of Popped Kernels

Helpful hint: Too many lines on a line graph can be confusing, especially if they overlap. Try to find the simplest graph that makes your point.

Pie Chart

Pie charts are used to show percentages or fractions. They are sometimes called circle graphs too. The whole circle (or pie) equals 100 percent and the different pieces of the pie make up the whole. Pie charts do not show changes over time. For example, you could use a pie chart to show what percentage of a bag of popcorn contained, popped, unpopped and burnt kernels. Be sure to include a title and a legend for deciphering the graph.

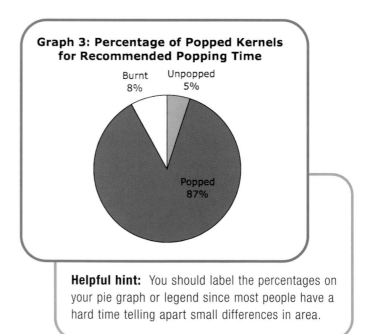

Graph 3: Percentage of Popped Kernels for Recommended Popping Time

Helpful hint: You should label the percentages on your pie graph or legend since most people have a hard time telling apart small differences in area.

The Projects

The projects in the next three chapters explore three major branches of science: biology, physical science, and chemistry.

If the project requires adult supervision or assistance, there will be an **ADULT SUPERVISION REQUIRED** icon at the top of the project page. Take this seriously. Science is a lot of fun, but you have to be careful.

Every experiment is broken down into different sections. Read the whole thing before deciding it's the project for you.

The **PROBLEM/PURPOSE** asks the question that the experiment will try to answer. Note that there is no section for the hypothesis. It's your job to do the research and come up with your own hypothesis.

The **EXPERIMENT SUMMARY** gives you a basic idea of how you'll conduct the experiment.

WHAT YOU NEED lists everything you'll need to do the experiment. Each list tells you how many volunteers, plant seeds, raw eggs, etc., you'll need to perform a valid experiment. Remember, however, that the more trials you perform, the more valid your results will be. So, find more volunteers, grow more plants, or smash more eggs whenever possible. Make sure you have everything on this list before you start your experiment.

The **EXPERIMENTAL PROCEDURE** gives you step-by-step instructions for performing the experiment.

The **CONCLUSION** provides questions, advice, and general assistance to help you find your conclusion.

For many of the projects, there's a section called **TAKE A CLOSER LOOK**. This section provides more information about the conclusion and often includes facts, tidbits, and other information that will help you with your research.

WHAT ELSE YOU CAN DO gives you ideas for similar experiments you can perform.

Biology

Biology is the science of living things, and there are a lot of living things out there to study. A typical science fair may have twice as many biology projects as physical science or chemistry. And it's easy to see why: plants can't run away from you, people are always interesting to study, animals are fascinating, bugs are fun, and mold is just plain cool. So if you've ever been curious about crickets, getting dizzy, dandelion seeds, eating food off the floor, where bugs live, how taste buds work, or making a self-sustaining biosphere, this chapter is for you.

Low Fat, Low Carb, Low Taste?

These days it seems everyone's on a diet. Cookie makers are taking advantage of people's search for low-fat, low-calorie, and low-carbohydrate sweets. But do these cookies taste as good as the real thing?

PROBLEM/PURPOSE

How does the diet-friendliness of a cookie affect its taste?

EXPERIMENT SUMMARY

You'll perform a taste test for a variety of diet and regular cookies.

WHAT YOU NEED

▶ **Marker**

▶ **Resealable plastic bags**

▶ **Several different diet sandwich cookies (low fat, low carb, low calorie, etc.) and regular sandwich cookies**

▶ **Paper and pencil**

▶ **Blindfold**

▶ **Several volunteers (at least 10)**

▶ **Glass of milk or water (optional)**

EXPERIMENTAL PROCEDURE

1. With the marker, label the plastic bags A, B, C, etc., depending on how many different types of cookies you have.

2. Empty one package of cookies into each bag and record on a separate piece paper which type of cookie corresponds to which letter. This will help you be unbiased when administering the test and make it more difficult for your volunteers to figure out the identity of the cookies.

3. Blindfold a volunteer. Give her one cookie at a time to taste. You may also want to provide a glass of milk or water to drink between cookies.

4. After tasting each cookie, ask the volunteer to rank each cookie from 1 (lowest/worst) to 5 (highest/best) for each of the following categories: texture, sweetness, crispness, and overall taste.

5. Repeat steps 3 and 4 with the rest of your volunteers.

6. Average the rankings in each of the categories for each of the cookies.

CONCLUSION

Which cookies rated highest in each of the four categories? Which cookie would you consider the overall winner? How did the diet cookies compare to the regular cookies? Were you or any of your volunteers surprised by the results? Look at the ingredient lists for the cookies. Do you see any similarities in the cookies that ranked high or low?

WHAT ELSE YOU CAN DO

Try testing other foods that have diet alternatives, such as popcorn, peanut butter, soda pop, or potato chips. What other categories could you use in your taste test? Investigate the different sugar and fat substitutes that these products use.

The Five-Second Rule

Have you ever dropped a chocolate chip cookie on the floor, quickly scooped it back up, and finished eating it? As everyone knows, if food is on the ground for less then 5 seconds, it's safe to eat. Isn't it?

PROBLEM/PURPOSE

How much does bacteria contaminate dry and wet food that has been dropped on the ground?

EXPERIMENT SUMMARY

You'll drop graham crackers and bananas on the floor for 5 seconds and take a bacterial culture to see whether the food is contaminated.

WHAT YOU NEED

- ▶ Permanent marker
- ▶ 12 sterile petri dishes*
- ▶ 1 cup (275.5 ml) distilled water
- ▶ Saucepan
- ▶ 1 tablespoon (14 g) unflavored gelatin**
- ▶ Beef bouillon cube
- ▶ Spoon
- ▶ Box of sterile gloves
- ▶ Unopened package of graham crackers***
- ▶ Unopened box of cotton swabs***
- ▶ Kitchen floor
- ▶ Stopwatch
- ▶ Banana
- ▶ Butter knife
- ▶ Resealable plastic bags
- ▶ Warm, dark location
- ▶ Notebook and pencil

You can get petri dishes from science supply companies.

** *Look for gelatin at the grocery store.*

*** *If the packages have been opened, your supplies may be contaminated by foreign bacteria.*

"5..4..3. . .got it. Still good!"

EXPERIMENTAL PROCEDURE

1. Use the permanent marker to label the bottom of three petri dishes "Undropped Cracker" and number them 1 through 3. Label three petri dishes "Undropped Banana" and number them 1 through 3. Label three petri dishes "Dropped Cracker" and number them 1 through 3. Label three petri dishes "Dropped Banana" and number them 1 through 3.

2. Like all living things, bacteria need a particular environment in which to thrive. To make a bacteria-friendly environment, pour 1 cup (275.5 ml) of distilled water into the saucepan. Bring the water to a boil and add the gelatin and beef bouillon cube to the water.

3. Stir the mixture constantly with the spoon until the gelatin and beef cube completely dissolve.

4. Carefully fill each of the petri dishes halfway with hot bacteria food. Immediately put the lids on the dishes. Let the petri dishes sit overnight so that the gelatin sets.

5. Put on a pair of the sterile gloves. Remove one graham cracker from the package and be careful not to let the package touch the cracker. (There may be bacteria on the outside of the package.) Remove one cotton swab from the package and be careful not to let the package touch the swab. (There may be bacteria on the outside of the package.) Brush the cotton swab across the

surface of the cracker and then gently glide it across the surface of the petri dish labeled "Undropped Cracker 1." Seal the lid.

"I did *not* just see that!"

6. Repeat step 5 with two more crackers, putting each sample in a separate petri dish. Put on a new pair of sterile gloves each time.

7. Put on a new pair of gloves. Carefully remove another graham cracker from the package and drop it on the kitchen floor. Leave it there for 5 seconds. Use the stopwatch to time it. (If your crackers keep breaking, gently place them on the floor.)

8. Pick up the graham cracker and use the cotton swab to swab the cracker. Then, gently glide the swab across the surface of the petri dish labeled "Dropped Cracker 1" and seal the dish.

9. Throw away the gloves and repeat steps 7 and 8 with two more crackers, putting each sample in a separate petri dish. Make sure you drop the food on a different part of the floor each time so that the crumbs from the crackers you've dropped won't affect your experiment.

10. Carefully peel the banana. Put on a new pair of sterile gloves and use the butter knife to slice off six pieces. Be careful not to let the banana touch the outside of the peel, the countertop, or anything that might contaminate it. Put the slices inside a resealable plastic bag.

11. Repeat steps 5 and 6 with three of the banana slices, sealing them in the appropriately labeled petri dishes.

12. Repeat steps 7, 8, and 9 using three slices of banana and sealing them in the appropriately labeled petri dishes.

13. Put all the petri dishes in a dark, warm area of your home. Closets, small rooms, and warm basements work well. Wash your hands with hot soapy water.

14. Check the dishes for bacterial growth every 12 hours for 5 days. Record any changes in the dishes. Note the color, size, and shape of the bacteria in each dish. Compare the differences between the dropped and undropped food dishes. If you'd like, you can photograph the dishes for your presentation. Whatever you do, don't open the lids.

15. After 5 days, record your final results. After all the data have been recorded, put the dishes in a resealable plastic bag and throw them away.

"Mmm. . . DELICIOUS!"

CONCLUSION

The undropped crackers and bananas are your control groups. Any growth on these dishes probably comes from naturally occurring bacteria on the crackers and bananas. (It could also be some sort of contamination that got in the petri dish when you weren't looking.) How does the bacteria growth on the dropped foods compare to that on the undropped foods? How does the bacteria growth on the dry graham cracker compare to that on the wet banana? Does food left on the floor for 5 seconds become contaminated?

TAKE A CLOSER LOOK

Up to one-third of the world's population suffers from food poisoning every year. Harmful *bacteria* that can only be seen with a microscope cause this problem. Harmful bacteria grow readily in foods at room temperature, especially meat, fish, and dairy products. These bacteria can make you sick, infecting cells in your intestinal tract and causing vomiting or diarrhea. There are also good types of bacteria, some of which make yogurt and cheese. Others decompose fallen leaves and trees in the forest, playing an important role in the health of the ecosystem.

WHAT ELSE YOU CAN DO

Try testing other foods or surfaces. Does the bathroom floor have more bacteria than the kitchen floor? How about your bedroom or the sidewalk outside your house? What if you left the food on the ground for longer than 5 seconds?

This experiment only tests contamination by bacteria that like gelatin and beef food best. Some bacteria prefer milk, sugar, or soy foods. Ask your science teacher to help you prepare the environments these bacteria need to thrive.

Hip to Be Square

It used to be an insult to call somebody a square. After you perform this experiment, you'll know it's not an insult—just good science.

PROBLEM/PURPOSE

How much more alike are two people's body dimensions if they are related than if they're just friends?

EXPERIMENT SUMMARY

You'll measure your dimensions and compare them to those of your family and friends.

MATERIALS

▶ **Tape measure**
▶ **Calculator**
▶ **Family members**
▶ **Friends**

EXPERIMENTAL PROCEDURE

1. With the tape measure, measure your height and wingspan. (Your wingspan is the distance from fingertip to fingertip when your arms are outstretched.)

2. To find the ratio of height to wingspan, use a calculator to divide your height by your wingspan. The closer this value is to 1, the squarer your body is. This is your *Square Factor*. Record this number.

3. Measure the height and wingspan of your family and friends. Calculate their Square Factor.

4. Average the Square Factors for the people related to you.

5. Calculate the average deviation for your Square Factor by subtracting the family average, which you figured out in step 4, from your Square Factor and dividing by the average. The average deviation shows how close together two or more numbers are. You will use this to see how close your Square Factor is to the rest of your family.

6. Repeat steps 4 and 5 for your friends to see how close your square factor is to people you aren't related to.

Forrest has a Square Factor of 1.10 because he is taller than his wingspan. His sister has a Square Factor of 1.15. To find the average deviation, subtract the two numbers: 1.15 - 1.10 = .05.

Then divide this number by the family average: .05 ÷ 1.15 = .04 or 4%

CONCLUSION

Compare the average deviation between you and your families' Square Factor to the average deviation between you and your friends' Square Factors. Which is smallest? The smallest average deviation will tell you which group of people, your family or your friends, has the closest average Square Factor to yours. Do you think body dimensions are inherited? What other factors might affect your Square Factor?

WHAT ELSE YOU CAN DO

Is your Square Factor closer to your Mom or Dad's Square Factor? Which parent do you think you look more like? What about your brothers or sisters?

What other body dimensions might be inherited? Compare the ratio of the width of your shoulders and the circumference of your neck, or the ratio of the length of your forearm and the length of your foot.

Fee Φ Fo Fum

You probably learned about *Pi* (π) in your math class when studying circles, but have you heard about *Phi* (Φ)? Like Pi, Phi is an irrational number that never ends (Φ = 1.6180339887....) but it shows up in some pretty crazy places, such as in your fingers and the dimensions of your parent's credit card.

Imagine your finger split into four parts. The tip of your finger to the first knuckle is the first part, followed by your first knuckle to your second knuckle, then your second knuckle to the third knuckle and then the third knuckle to your wrist. If you were to measure each section, you would find that each of the parts is about Φ longer than the previous! In fact your forearm is also about Φ times longer than the length of your hand. So if your hand is 6 inches (15.2 cm) long, then your forearm should be about 9.5 inches (24.1 cm) long (6 inches x 1.618=9.5).

The human face also contains Φ. The face can be broken into rectangles. One side of the rectangle is Φ longer than the other. This is called the *golden rectangle*. Your head forms a golden rectangle with your eyes in the middle. In other words, your head is Φ longer than it is wide.

Even your teeth form golden rectangles. Look at your two front teeth together as a rectangle. This rectangle is Φ wider than it is tall.

A golden section is $\frac{1}{\Phi}$ of a distance. For example, your mouth is located $\frac{1}{\Phi}$ times the distance from your eyes to your chin, from your eyes. If your eyes were higher or lower, your face would just look funny. Our eyes automatically recognize golden rectangles as being more pleasing to look at. Artists have known this for centuries and if you study paintings by Picasso, de Vinci and others you'll find golden rectangles all over the place. Nature is in on the action as well. Your body, snail shells, flowers, trees, animals and even DNA are made of golden rectangles.

eyes are at the midsection

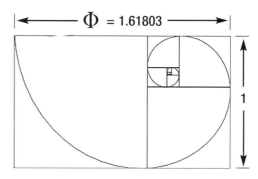

Φ = 1.61803

1

The Golden Rectangle

Reaching for the Light

If you watch a field of sunflowers, you'll see them turn to follow the path of the sun throughout the day. Do other plants do this, too?

PROBLEM/PURPOSE

How does light affect the leaf positions of bean seedlings?

EXPERIMENT SUMMARY

You'll observe the position of bean leaves at different times of day to measure the leaf's cycle. Then you'll modify the light conditions and observe the effect on the bean leaf's cycle.

WHAT YOU NEED

- ▶ Scissors
- ▶ 12 paper cups
- ▶ Potting soil
- ▶ 12 lima beans
- ▶ Water
- ▶ Sunny window
- ▶ Notebook and pencil
- ▶ Camera (optional)
- ▶ Dark cupboard
- ▶ 2 gooseneck lamps

EXPERIMENTAL PROCEDURE

1. Use the scissors to cut a small hole in the bottom of each of the cups. These holes will allow excess water to drain out.

2. Fill the cups with potting soil and plant a lima bean about 1 inch (2.5 cm) deep in each one. Water the cups so the soil is moist and place them in a bright sunny window. Monitor the cups throughout the experiment to make sure the soil does not dry out. The bean seeds will take two to three weeks to sprout and develop leaves. Make sure you take this into account when setting up a timeline for your experiment.

3. After the bean plants have developed leaves, observe the position of the leaves every 4 hours for 48 hours. (Plan to do this over a weekend.) The leaves will either be up, down, or somewhere in between. Record the time and the position of the leaves. You can use a camera to take pictures for your display.

4. Place three of the plants in a dark cupboard, three plants under a lamp that is on all day and all night, and three plants under a lamp that is turned on and off every 8 hours (making a 16-hour day). Leave the remaining three plants in the sunny window.

5. Leave the plants in their new conditions for 48 hours. Then repeat step 3 for all 12 plants

CONCLUSION

Make a graph of the average leaf positions of the 12 plants in the sunny window. Make graphs of the average leaf positions of the plants in continuous dark, continuous light, and the 16-hour days. How did the pattern of leaf position change when you moved the plants?

TAKE A CLOSER LOOK

Biological clocks are internal systems that control the timing of different activities. In the bean plants, the leaves change position to control photosynthesis and conserve moisture. The plants run on a cycle of about 24 hours, which is called a *circadian rhythm*. *Circa* comes from the Latin word meaning "around" and *dian* comes from the word "a day." Even if the bean plants lived in the dark and couldn't tell what time it was, the leaves would keep going on the 24-hour cycle.

WHAT ELSE YOU CAN DO

How does temperature affect the bean plant's biological clock? Compare the movements of plants in a cool temperature with those in a warm temperature. Does the type of light a plant receives affect its cycle? Try using different types of lightbulbs in the lamp and compare them with sunlight.

Aquatic Bottle Biosphere

In order for humans to live in space stations, there has to be a contained environment to provide air and water. These contained environments are called *biospheres*. If a biosphere is able to survive without any outside support, such as air or food, it is said to be self-sustaining.

PROBLEM/PURPOSE

What role do plants play in making a self-sustaining closed aquatic biosphere?

EXPERIMENT SUMMARY

You'll create aquatic bottle biospheres with water, snails, water fleas, and different numbers of plants to observe which biospheres are self-sustaining.

WHAT YOU NEED

- ▶ **10 liters of spring water**
- ▶ **5 empty 2-liter soda bottles**
- ▶ **Permanent marker**
- ▶ **10 aquatic plants of the same size and species***
- ▶ **Paper towels**
- ▶ **Ruler**
- ▶ **Scale**
- ▶ **Notebook and pencil**
- ▶ **Spoon**
- ▶ **Aquarium gravel***
- ▶ **25 water fleas (Daphnia magna)***
- ▶ **5 snails***
- ▶ **Camera (optional)**

* You can find these supplies at an aquarium store.

EXPERIMENTAL PROCEDURE

1. Set the bottles of spring water out on a counter overnight so they'll reach room temperature. (Warm or cold water may kill the water fleas and snails.)

2. Rinse the empty soda bottles well with clean warm water to remove any soda. Don't use soap! Any soap residue in the bottles will be harmful to the water fleas and snails. Let the bottles dry.

3. With the marker, label the bottles 0, 1, 2, 3, and 4.

4. Set bottle 0 aside. You won't put any plants in this bottle.

5. Pat the first plant dry with a paper towel. Measure it with the ruler and weigh it on the scale. Record the data.

6. Put the plant in Bottle 1 and use a spoon to add an inch (2.5 cm) of gravel to the bottle. This will anchor the plant to the bottom of the bottle.

7. Fill the bottle half full with the spring water.

8. Use the spoon to add five water fleas to the bottle. Add one snail to the bottle as well.

9. Add more spring water to the bottle. Leave 3 to 4 inches (7.6 to 10.2 cm) of empty space at the top. Tightly screw the cap onto the bottle.

10. Repeat steps 5 through 9, adding two plants to Bottle 2, three plants to Bottle 3, four plants to Bottle 4, and no plants to Bottle 0. For each bottle with multiple plants, add up the weights of all the plants in the bottle and record the total.

11. Place the bottles in a cool spot away from direct sunlight. Do not place the bottles in the dark. The plants need some light but not so much that it heats up the water.

12. Observe the bottles each day. Be sure to count the water fleas (if you can find them all) and record any changes in the plants, snail, or water. The number of water fleas may increase if they reproduce. You may want to take photos of the bottles in case there are subtle changes you don't notice from day to day.

13. After a week (or longer if your bottles continue to flourish) make a final count of the water fleas in each bottle. Record the data.

14. Remove the plants from each bottle and pat them dry. Measure and weigh them again. Record the data.

CONCLUSION

Make a graph of the number of plants versus the number of water fleas. Did any of the bottles see an increase in water fleas? Did any see a decrease? What happened to the snail in each bottle? How did the weight of the plants after you removed them compare to the weight before? Did any of the plants grow while they were in the bottle? How did the number of water fleas change in the bottles with plant growth? Based on your data, what is the best number of plants to use in an aquatic bottle biosphere?

TAKE A CLOSER LOOK

For a biosphere to be self-sustaining there has to be a balance of resources. In your bottle biosphere, the plants provide oxygen for the water fleas, which then produce carbon dioxide for the plants. Waste from the snail and water fleas provide nutrients for the plants. The plants provide food for the snail, and the water fleas feed on microscopic algae that grow on the leaves of the plants and in the water. If the resources aren't balanced, the biosphere won't thrive.

WHAT ELSE YOU CAN DO

Use an aquarium water test kit to monitor the water quality of your biosphere each day. Try changing other variables, such as temperature, light, or the amount of air at the top of the bottle. What happens when you add fertilizer or an herbicide to your biospheres? What if you added a different number of snails to each bottle? Try other combinations of plants and creatures in your bottles. Check your science fair rules on the use of vertebrates if you would like to try guppies or other fish. What would happen if you used different species of plants?

"Outta my way . . .
I'm heading to the biosphere."

Take a Spin

Some people really like feeling dizzy and others avoid it as much as they can. What does it take to get dizzy?

How does someone's gender affect how long it takes to get dizzy?

EXPERIMENT SUMMARY

You'll spin volunteers around on a chair to figure out how long it takes them to get dizzy.

WHAT YOU NEED

▶ **10 or more male and female volunteers**
▶ **Blindfold**
▶ **Chair that spins**
▶ **Stopwatch (optional)**

EXPERIMENTAL PROCEDURE

1. Choose one of your volunteers to be spun first. Have her sit in the chair, then put the blindfold on her. Record her gender.

2. Quickly spin your volunteer around. After one complete rotation, carefully stop the chair so that she doesn't fall off. Ask her whether she feels as if she is stopped or moving.

If she says moving, ask her in which direction. Record her answers and the number of times you spun her.

3. If your volunteer feels as if she is still moving, let her sit still for 1 minute or until any dizziness wears off.

4. Repeat steps 2 and 3, increasing the number of spins by one each time until your volunteer still feels as if she's moving when the chair stops. (Instead of counting the number of spins, you could use the stopwatch and spin your volunteers for different intervals of time.)

5. Repeat steps 1 through 4 for at least nine other volunteers.

CONCLUSION

What was the average number of spins it took for your volunteers to get dizzy? When did they feel like they were still moving? Was the direction they thought they were turning the same as the direction the chair was actually turning? Did you see any patterns related to gender?

TAKE A CLOSER LOOK

The root of dizziness lies in your inner ear. Only a small part of the inner ear, called the *cochlea*, actually helps you hear. The rest of the inner ear contains three semicircular canals, which primarily detect how your head moves. The canals are filled with a watery fluid and contain a projection, like a swinging door, called the *cupola*. The cupola senses the motion of the fluid.

When you're not moving, the fluid isn't moving. As you spin around on the chair, the fluid starts to flow through the canals and pushes the cupola open. Once you've been spinning for a while, your head, the canals, and the fluid are all moving together. The cupola swings back down. At this point, you don't feel like you're moving, even though you really are. When your head and the canals stop spinning, the fluid keeps moving and pushes the cupola open the other way. This gives you the sensation of spinning in the opposite direction. If you remove your blindfold, your brain gets confused because your ears say you're moving but your eyes say you're still. This is being dizzy.

Inner Ear or Labyrinth

Cupola

Semicircular Canals

Eardrum

Cochlea

WHAT ELSE YOU CAN DO

How can you get undizzy? Try turning your volunteer a quarter or half a turn in the opposite direction immediately after spinning. If your volunteer is sitting still, how much time does it take for the dizziness to go away? If your volunteer is spinning quickly on the chair, can she tell whether the chair slows down? Be sure to test out your ideas on several volunteers.

Follow That Tree

You're lost in a deep, dark forest. You know you need to walk north to get back to town, but you have no compass. The bark on the trees is covered with all sorts of growing stuff, including moss, lichen, and algae. Will this help you find your way out of the woods?

PROBLEM/PURPOSE

How is the organism growth on a tree affected by direction?

EXPERIMENT SUMMARY

You'll record the organism growth and the side of the tree it grows on to see whether the factors influence each other.

WHAT YOU NEED

▶ **Several trees**
▶ **Compass**
▶ **Wire coat hanger**
▶ **Yardstick**
▶ **Masking tape**
▶ **Paper and pencil**
▶ **Camera (optional)**

EXPERIMENTAL PROCEDURE

1. Find several trees of the same type in the same area. Make sure that the lowest branches are higher than you can reach, and avoid young trees with skinny trunks. (This will ensure good organism growth on the trees and that they'll be big enough for you to obtain data from different sides.)

2. Record your observations about the position of the sun at 8:00 A.M., 12:00 P.M., and 4:00 P.M. Use your compass to determine the direction of the sun at those times.

3. Bend your coat hanger into a square. You'll use this to define the area on the tree trunk where you make your observations.

4. Use the compass to figure out which part of the trunk faces North.

5. Measure 1 yard (.9 m) up the North-facing part of the trunk. Tape the wire square to the tree. (The bottom of it should be 1 yard [.9 m] off the ground.)

6. Carefully observe the growth you see inside the square. *Lichens* can look like a crust, small leaves, or shrubs. The colors are gray, orange-black, or blue-green. (Lichens are actually two organisms: an alga and a fungus growing in a symbiotic relationship.) *Algae* look like a bright green powdery covering. *Mosses* look like tiny green plants. Draw a sketch or take a photograph of what you see. Estimate the percentage cover of each type of organism.

7. Repeat steps 4 through 6 for the South, West, and East sides of the tree trunk.

8. Repeat steps 4 through 6 for the other trees you found in step 1.

CONCLUSION

What types of organisms did you find growing on the tree bark? Describe the average coverage on each side of the trees. Calculate the average percentage of each type of growth on each side of the tree. Did any organisms grow on only certain sides of the tree? How does this relate to the direction of the sun throughout the day? Can trees be used as directional compasses?

TAKE A CLOSER LOOK

Tree bark protects the inside of the tree and also provides a home for other organisms, such as moss, lichen, and algae. However, tree bark is a harsh environment in which to grow. It provides little water and dries out quickly in direct sunlight. For this reason, the organisms usually grow on the parts of the tree that receive the least amount of sunlight.

WHAT ELSE YOU CAN DO

Do other types of trees act as directional compasses? How does the bark growth on trees compare in the summer and winter? Find an identification book to identify the different species of lichen, algae, and moss you observe.

Taste Buds

Place some salt on the very tip of your tongue. Do you taste it? How about sugar? Our taste buds are built specifically for different tastes—sweet, salty, sour, and bitter—but exactly where these are located on the tongue can be different for every person.

PROBLEM/PURPOSE

How is your tongue's ability to taste different flavors affected by where you place food on it?

EXPERIMENT SUMMARY

You'll make a taste bud map of the tongue to several volunteers.

WHAT YOU NEED

▶ **Measuring spoons**
▶ **Sugar**
▶ **2 glasses**
▶ **Water**
▶ **Salt**
▶ **Paper and pencil**
▶ **5 or more volunteers**
▶ **Blindfold**
▶ **Toothpicks**
▶ **Lemon juice**
▶ **Tonic water**

EXPERIMENTAL PROCEDURE

1. Stir 3 tablespoons of sugar into a glass of water.

2. Stir 3 tablespoons of salt into another glass of water.

3. On a piece of paper, draw a large tongue shape for each volunteer. Record the age and gender of each volunteer. You'll record your data on the drawing. Make symbols for sweet, salty, sour, bitter, and no taste so that you don't have to write out the words.

4. Explain to your first volunteer that you're going to touch different parts of his tongue with either a sweet, salty, sour, or bitter flavor and you would like him to tell you what he tastes. Blindfold him.

5. Dip a toothpick into the salty water and lightly touch the tip of the tongue. Record the taste, if any, that the volunteer reports. It's all right if he reports no taste at all.

6. Test other parts of his tongue with the salty water. It may help to let the volunteer drink some plain water between tests. Be careful testing the back part of the tongue, because some people may gag.

7. Repeat the process, using a new toothpick each time, for the sugary water, the lemon juice (sour), and the tonic water (bitter). Be careful not to bias your volunteer by telling him what flavor you're testing.

8. Repeat steps 4 through 7 for the other volunteers.

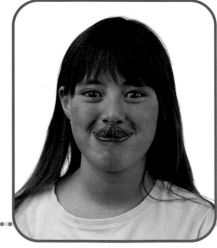

CONCLUSION

Are parts of the tongue more sensitive to specific flavors, or are all parts of the tongue equally sensitive to the flavors? Compare the tongue maps from all of the volunteers. Are there any similarities between boys and girls? How about people who are related?

TAKE A CLOSER LOOK

Our tongues actually detect five flavors: sweet, salty, sour, bitter, and *umami*. Umami is described as savoriness and has been known to Asian cultures for centuries, but scientists have only recently found a receptor, or taste bud, for it.

Contrary to popular belief, you can sense all tastes on all parts of the tongue. Each of your taste buds can perceive more than one flavor to varying degrees. This means there isn't just one part of your tongue that tastes sweet or salty. However, taste buds that are especially sensitive to bitter tastes, which happen to be found in many poisons, appear to be abundant at the back of the tongue, which controls your gag reflex. Why do you think that might be?

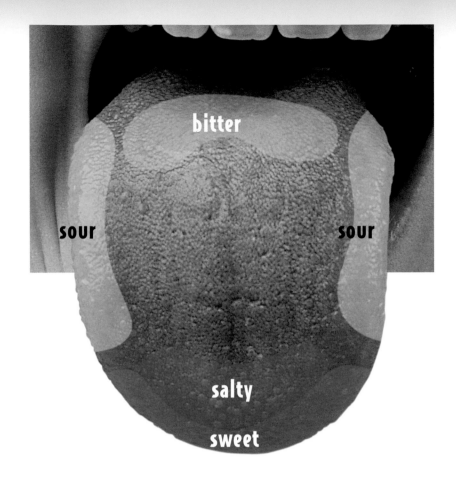

WHAT ELSE YOU CAN DO

Try using other foods or liquids to test for taste. How salty or sweet does something need to be before you can taste it? How does the ability to taste vary with age? How does your sense of taste change when you're sick?

Buggin' Out

Everybody needs a home—even the creepiest, crawliest insects. Tree bark provides all sorts of nooks and crannies for them to live in.

PROBLEM/PURPOSE

How does the type of tree bark affect the kinds of insects that live there?

EXPERIMENT SUMMARY

You'll collect insects from different types of trees at night using honey and a bug trap.

WHAT YOU NEED

- ▶ **Several different large trees, each with a different type of bark**
- ▶ **Tree identification book**
- ▶ **Notebook and pencil**
- ▶ **Scissors**
- ▶ **1 piece of cardboard for each tree, 12 x 18 inches (30.5 cm x 45.7 cm)**
- ▶ **String**
- ▶ **Knife**
- ▶ **Honey**
- ▶ **White poster board or sheet**
- ▶ **Large box**
- ▶ **Tweezers or forceps**
- ▶ **Insect identification book**

EXPERIMENTAL PROCEDURE

1. Find several different large trees with different types of bark. Use the tree guide to identify each type of tree you test. Record this information and describe the type of bark on each tree, such as papery or rough.

2. To make the insect traps, use scissors to cut holes in two corners of the long side of the cardboard. Tie a piece of string to each hole.

3. Repeat step 2, making a cardboard trap for each tree you'll be testing.

4. At dusk, set the traps. Use a knife to spread a thin layer of honey in the center of the cardboard.

5. Tie the cardboard to one of the trees you found in step 1, with the honey side against the bark. The cardboard should loosely fit the tree, so you may need to bend the sides a little.

6. Repeat steps 4 and 5 for each tree.

7. In the morning, put a piece of white poster board or a white sheet in the bottom of the large box. Place the box at the bottom of the first tree.

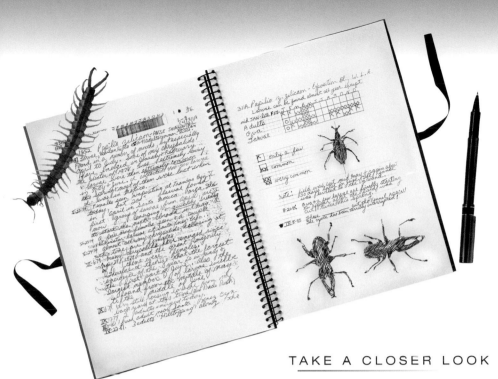

8. Carefully remove the trap from the tree. You want as many insects as possible to fall into the box or stick to the honey on the trap.

9. Use the tweezers or forceps to sort and count the bugs.

10. With the insect identification book, classify as many bugs as possible. Record the numbers and types of bugs you find on each tree.

CONCLUSION

Make a chart of the numbers and type of insects found on each tree. What relationships do you notice between bug type and tree type? What about between bug numbers and tree type? Based on the type of bark on the trees, do your conclusions make sense?

TAKE A CLOSER LOOK

Like people, some insects need a place to rest at night. They hide in the bark of trees to protect themselves from predators and the dew that settles at night. Different types of bark are ideal for different types of insects. The papery bark of birch and aspen trees provides refuge for the smallest insects, while the rougher bark of oak and pine trees can shelter beetles and larger bugs because they fit better.

WHAT ELSE YOU CAN DO

Compare the types and numbers of bugs found on nights with different temperatures or humidities. What about using other types of bait, such as peanut butter, rotting fruit, or nothing at all? Do the phases of the moon affect the number and type of insects you find?

The Time is Ripe

You've picked out what looks like the perfect pear. Your mouth is watering as you imagine how good it's going to taste. You take your first bite and—ouch! It's as hard as a rock! How can you make fruit ripen more quickly?

PROBLEM/PURPOSE

How do ripe apples affect the time it takes a pear to ripen?

EXPERIMENT SUMMARY

You'll store pears in paper bags with ripe apples to see which pears ripen first.

WHAT YOU NEED

▶ Marker
▶ 12 paper lunch bags
▶ 12 unripe pears
▶ 12 ripe apples
▶ Masking tape

"Eww. . . I didn't want to eat a rock for lunch!

EXPERIMENTAL PROCEDURE

1. With the marker, label four bags "Pear," four bags "Pear & One Apple," and four bags "Pear & Two Apples."

2. Place the pears and apples in the appropriate bags, roll down the tops, and seal them with tape.

3. Record the date and time you placed the fruit in the bags. You may want to write this on the bag.

4. Every 12 hours, check the pears for ripeness. To do this, press on the side of each pear firmly with your finger for 2 seconds. If the fruit remains indented after you remove your finger, then it's ripe. If you can't see where you pressed, put the fruit back and reseal the bag.

5. Record the time and date each pear ripens.

6. Calculate the average time it takes the pears to ripen in all three combinations.

CONCLUSION

Make a graph of average ripening time versus number of apples in the bag. Did the apples help the pears ripen more quickly? Was there much difference in the three combinations of fruit? How long do you think it would take if there were three or four apples in the bag?

TAKE A CLOSER LOOK

When fruits ripen, they release a chemical called *ethylene*. The presence of ethylene can cause other fruit to start ripening. Here, the ethylene given off by the apples caused the pears to ripen sooner than if they were left by themselves. Most fruits and vegetables you buy at the grocery store are actually picked and shipped before they're ripe. When fruit arrives at the store, the grocers spray it with ethylene to speed up the ripening process. This is why the tomatoes are always the perfect shade of red even though they may have been shipped hundreds or even thousands of miles.

It's important to use paper bags as well. The ethylene molecule is too big to escape through the bag, but oxygen can flow freely in and out. Oxygen keeps the fruit from rotting.

This experiment also shows the truth in the saying "One rotten apple will spoil the bunch." Long ago, apples were stored in large barrels in a cool cellar so they could be eaten year–round. If an overripe or rotten apple made it into the barrel, it would give off ethylene, causing the rest of the apples to ripen too quickly, and they rotted before they were eaten.

WHAT ELSE YOU CAN DO

What other combinations of ripe and unripe fruit could you use? What happens if you don't seal the paper bags or use something else, such as plastic, to hold the fruit? What effect does temperature have on the ripening of fruit?

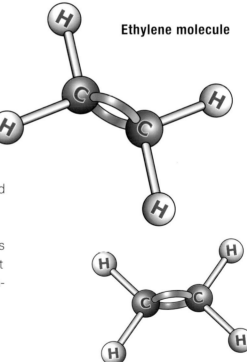

Ethylene molecule

Weather Warnings

Nature gives us all kinds of warnings about weather that's coming. Some people look at the groundhog's shadow to see when spring is coming and watch for wooly caterpillars to see how much snow we'll get. Supposedly, you can tell the temperature from listening to crickets chirping. How accurate is a cricket thermometer?

PROBLEM/PURPOSE

How is a cricket's chirping affected by temperature?

EXPERIMENT
SUMMARY

You'll measure a cricket's chirps at different temperatures and compare the measurements to the actual temperature.

WHAT YOU NEED

▶ **5 crickets***

▶ **5 shoeboxes**

▶ **Grass or leaves**

▶ **Stopwatch**

▶ **Thermometer**

* You can get crickets at pet stores. Young crickets won't chirp.

Chirp Chirp...
Chirp... Chirp... Chirp

(Translation: "There's a storm comin'!!")

EXPERIMENTAL
PROCEDURE

1. Put each cricket into a separate shoebox with some grass or leaves.

2. Take your crickets outside early in the morning. Using the stopwatch, wait 10 minutes for the crickets to adjust to the temperature.

3. Using the stopwatch, count the number of chirps each cricket makes in 15 seconds. Measure each cricket separately. Record the number of chirps.

4. Measure the air temperature with the thermometer.

5. Repeat steps 2 through 4 during other parts of the day when the temperature is higher or lower. You should try to get chirp counts for at least six different temperatures. You can measure inside or outside. Don't place your crickets in the oven or refrigerator. They might get hurt.

6. Average the number of chirps the crickets made at each temperature. Don't forget to let the crickets go.

CONCLUSION

Make a graph of the average number of chirps versus temperature. Do you see a pattern? The story is that adding 38 to the number of chirps in 15 seconds will give the air temperature in Farenheit. Try this for your data. Does it work?

TAKE A CLOSER LOOK

If any critter, from insects to people, gets too hot or too cold, its body systems won't function correctly. In order to survive, you have to be able to warm or cool yourself. People do this by sweating and shivering. Crickets can't do either. They move their legs and wings to regulate their temperature. This movement causes the chirping sound. As the temperature rises, they move their legs and wings to cool down, so the rate of chirping increases.

WHAT ELSE YOU CAN DO

What other factors, such as light, food, and water, affect the chirping frequency of a cricket?

Other animals and plants give weather clues as well. Some respond to changes in air pressure. When storms approach, the air pressure drops. This makes it more difficult for birds to fly, so they tend to roost when the pressure is low. Pinecones respond to lower pressure by opening up. Try observing birds and pinecones during fair and stormy weather. Measure the air pressure with a barometer and compare it to the behavior of those animals and plants.

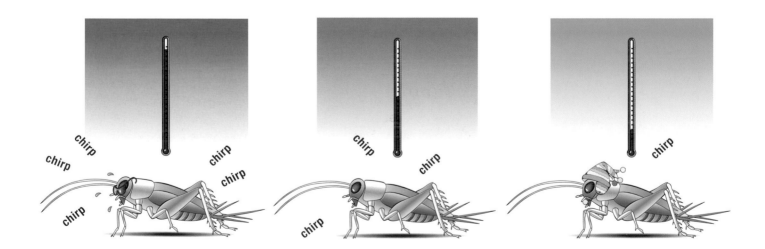

Stroop Effect

Look at the words below. Try naming the color of each word. Be careful! You're trying to say the color, not the word.

RED   YELLOW   BLUE   GREEN   RED   ORANGE   YELLOW   BLACK

Does your brain hurt? You've just experienced the Stroop Effect.

PROBLEM/PURPOSE

How does age affect the time it takes to complete a Stroop Effect test?

EXPERIMENT SUMMARY

You'll give volunteers of different ages a Stroop Effect test and compare their times.

WHAT YOU NEED

▶ **Crayons or colored markers**

▶ **Paper or card stock**

▶ **Volunteers of various ages***

▶ **Stopwatch**

* Make sure all of your volunteers can read and no one is color-blind.

EXPERIMENTAL PROCEDURE

1. With the crayons or markers, write each color word with the same color marker, for example, **RED** Label these cards "Test 1."

2. On the other pieces of paper, write each color word with a different colored marker, for example, **GREEN**. Label these cards "Test 2."

3. Take your first volunteer into a separate room. Record the age of your volunteer.

4. Explain that you would like your volunteer to name the color of each of the words you show him. With a stopwatch, measure and record the time from when you first show him Test Card 1 to when he finishes naming the colors of the words.

5. Next, show the volunteer Test Card 2. Measure and record the time from when you first show him the card to when he finishes naming the colors of the words. If the volunteer names the wrong color, wait until he names the right one.

6. Calculate the difference in the time it took to complete both tests by subtracting the time to read the colors on the Test 1 card from the time for the Test 2 card.

7. Repeat steps 3 through 6 for each of your volunteers.

CONCLUSION

Make a graph of age versus average time for Test 1, Test 2, and the difference between the two tests. Do you see a pattern? Is there a relationship between age and performance on the Stroop Effect tests? What other observations did you make about the volunteers while they took the Stroop Effect tests?

TAKE A CLOSER LOOK

The Stroop Effect is named after J. Ridley Stroop, who discovered this strange phenomenon in the 1930s. He found that the words have a strong influence on your ability to say the color. The interference between the different information (what the words say and the color of the words) your brain receives causes a problem. There are two theories that may explain the Stroop Effect. *The Speed of Processing Theory* states that the interference occurs because the words are read faster than the colors are named. *The Selective Attention Theory* states that the interference occurs because naming colors requires more attention than reading words. Which do you think is right? Why do you think that?

WHAT ELSE YOU CAN DO

Test young kids who know their colors but can't read yet. Try other tests, such as turning the words upside down or sideways, writing the words backward, using noncolor words such as "dog" or "house," or using nonsense words such as "blig" or "lowk." Design an experiment to test if gender affects performance.

blig

yellow

wolley

lowk

orange

neerg

The Weed Seed Freeze

Have you ever picked a dandelion that's going to seed and made a wish before blowing the seeds off? The seeds are scattered in the summer, and, after even the harshest winter, dandelions pop up again in the spring.

PROBLEM/PURPOSE

What factors will prevent dandelion seeds from germinating?

EXPERIMENT SUMMARY

You'll subject dandelion seeds to winterlike conditions and test whether the seeds are still able to germinate.

WHAT YOU NEED

► Several dandelion plants that have gone to seed
► 5 resealable plastic bags
► Masking tape
► Permanent marker
► Freezer
► 2 glasses
► Salt
► Water
► Spoon
► Paper towels
► 5 small plates

EXPERIMENTAL PROCEDURE

1. Collect and pull apart two dandelion "puffballs." Separate the hard, brown seeds from the white fluff.

2. Divide the seeds into five piles of 25 seeds each. Seal each pile in a separate plastic bag.

3. Use the masking tape and permanent marker to label one of the plastic bags "frozen five days." Put the bag in the freezer.

4. After four days, label another plastic bag of seeds "frozen one day" and put it in the freezer.

5. On the fifth day, fill a glass about one-third full with salt and the rest of the way with warm water. Stir the mixture with a spoon until the salt is dissolved. Set the glass aside for 30 minutes. The salt solution will simulate the effect of using salt to melt snow in the winter may have on germination.

6. Soak a paper towel with water, and wring it out so that it's moist but not dripping. Fold the paper towel so it fits on the plate. Spread 25 seeds from another plastic bag evenly on the paper towel. Place the dish in a new plastic bag and seal it. With the tape and marker, label this bag "control."

7. Place the control dish where it will get good light but not direct sunlight. You don't want the seeds to get too warm.

8. Wet and wring out two paper towels and put them on two plates.

9. Remove the seeds from the freezer. Spread the seeds that were frozen overnight evenly on one plate, bag it, and label it "frozen one day." Spread the seeds that were frozen five days evenly on the other plate, bag it, and label it "frozen five days." Set these two plates with the control.

10. Pour a bit of the saturated salt solution you made in step 5 into another glass so that the glass is about one-quarter full. Fill it the rest of the way with warm water and stir it. Soak a towel in this solution and then put it on a plate. Spread 25 seeds from the fourth plastic bag evenly on the towel, bag it, and label it "diluted salt solution." Place it with the other plates.

11. Soak a paper towel in the saturated salt solution you made in step 5 and then put it on a plate. Spread 25 seeds from the last plastic bag evenly on the plate, bag it, and label it "concentrated salt solution." Place it with the other plates.

12. Check the moisture of the towels every two days to make sure they don't dry out. Add a little water if necessary.

13. After five days, count and record the number of seeds that have germinated on each plate. You should see roots and leaves coming out of the germinated seeds.

14. After ten days, count and record the number of seeds germinated on each plate again.

15. Determine the percentage of seeds germinated at five days and at 10 days on each plate, and record these figures on a data table. To calculate the percentage of germinated seeds, divide the number of seeds germinated on a plate by the number of seeds planted (25). Then multiply this number by 100 to express your answer as a percentage.

CONCLUSION

How did the two salt solutions affect the percentage of seeds germinated? Compare this with the control. How did freezing the seeds for a day affect germination? How did freezing the seeds for five days affect the number of seeds germinated at five and ten days? What do your results suggest about the adaptation of dandelions to winter climates? What was the percentage germinated in the control? Did you find any conditions under which dandelion seeds did not germinate? If so, could these be used to prevent the rapid spread of dandelions in your lawn?

TAKE A CLOSER LOOK

Dandelions are one of the most common plants in North America. They're generally considered weeds, although some people eat the leaves in salad or as a cooked vegetable. Dandelion germination is actually improved by a cold period. This is true of many plants that grow in climates where there is a winter season. The seeds germinate as well or better after being frozen, demonstrating their adaptation to a cold climate. The seeds germinate poorly or not at all in the salt solutions. Salt is sometimes used to melt snow during the winter. Dandelions might not survive high levels of contact with saltwater runoff. Will other plants survive salted soil?

WHAT ELSE YOU CAN DO

How does extreme heat and dryness affect the germination of seeds? Try baking the seeds for 30 minutes instead of freezing them. What types of soils are best (or worst) for the survival of dandelions? Try testing the seeds of other plants that are considered weeds.

Pumping Iron

When you exercise or lift weights, you start breathing quickly and you get really warm. Why is this?

PROBLEM/PURPOSE

How does using your muscles affect your heart rate and temperature?

EXPERIMENT SUMMARY

You'll exercise different muscles while recording their temperature and your heart rate.

WHAT YOU NEED

▸**Stopwatch**

▸**Helper**

▸**Digital thermometer**

▸**Ankle weight and free weight, between 3 and 5 pounds each (1.4 kg and 2.3 kg)**

EXPERIMENTAL PROCEDURE

1. Practice measuring your heart rate. Place your index and middle fingers on your neck a couple of inches below your ear and just behind your jawbone. You should feel a pulsing just below your skin. This is the blood moving through your arteries as your heart pumps blood. Each pulse is a contraction of your heart. Use the stopwatch to count how many pulses you feel in 10 seconds. This is your heart rate. You should have about 10 to 15 pulses in 10 seconds (or 60 to 90 beats per minute) if you're sitting still. Practice finding and recording your pulse until you feel comfortable measuring your heart rate.

2. Have your helper place the tip of the thermometer against the middle of your bicep for 1 minute. (This will give the thermometer enough time to measure your muscle's temperature.) Keep the thermometer on your muscle and record its initial value.

3. Take your heart rate. Record this as your starting heart rate.

4. Hold the weight in your hand and begin exercising your bicep by doing curls. (See the chart on page 45 for exercises.)

5. After 30 seconds, have your helper take the temperature of your muscle while you take your heart rate. Record the data.

6. Repeat step 5, exercising and taking measurements in 30 second intervals until you've exercised your bicep for 3 minutes.

7. Stop exercising and continue to record your muscle temperature and heart rate every 30 seconds until you return to your starting values.

8. Repeat steps 2 through 6 for other muscles, including your triceps, quadriceps, and abdominal muscles.

CONCLUSION

Make a graph for each muscle, charting the temperature and heart rate versus time from just before you started exercising until your heart rate returned to normal. Is there any correlation between heart rate and temperature? What sorts of patterns, if any, do you see? When is the heart rate highest? When is the temperature highest? How do the recovery times compare for the different muscles?

TAKE A CLOSER LOOK

When you exercise, your body uses the oxygen you breathe to convert the chemicals in your cells into energy. However, your body doesn't use this energy very efficiently. Only 25 percent of the energy produced is used to do work—in this case to lift the weight. The other 75 percent is converted into heat. This is what makes your muscles, as well as the rest of your body, heat up.

Your heart pumps blood to your muscles. The blood carries the oxygen your cells need to produce energy. When you exercise, you use up the oxygen quickly, so your heart has to beat faster to keep the blood flowing to your muscle.

WHAT ELSE YOU CAN DO

Compare muscle and heart rate changes in boys and girls or in children and adults. Does it matter what time of day you perform the experiment or what the temperature of the room is? How about on an empty or a full stomach? What changes would using a heavier or lighter weight make? How about the speed at which you lift the weight? How do other exercises, such as bicycling or rowing, affect heart rate and muscle temperature? Is the temperature or heart rate affected by the size of the muscle being exercised? Measure your body temperature with a second thermometer in your mouth. Compare this to your muscle temperatures.

Muscle and Exercise

Bicep: Put the weight in your hand and stand with your elbow near your waist. Your arm should make a right angle at your elbow. Keep the top part of your arm still and raise the weight up toward your shoulder and then back down.

Tricep: Hold the weight in your hand and raise it high above your head. Keeping the bottom part of your arm still, bend at the elbow to lower the weight behind your head. Slowly raise the weight straight up.

Quadricep: Strap the ankle weight to your ankle and sit in a chair with your knees bent. Raise your foot until your leg is straight. Then return it to the ground.

Upper abdominal muscles: Lay on your back with your legs bent and feet flat on the ground. Place your hands behind your head to support your neck. Pull your shoulders up off the ground while squeezing the muscles in your stomach.

Lower abdominal muscles: Lay flat on the ground with your legs out straight. Put your hands under your tailbone to provide support for your lower back. Hold both feet 6 inches (15.2 cm) off the ground and extend them straight up and then back down.

Physical Science

If biology is the study of life, then physical science is the study of everything that's not alive. This topic covers nature, weather, water, magnets, stars, planets, environmental concerns, engineering, physics, and more. If you've ever wondered about how sound travels, magnetic fields work, coins flip, kites fly, gym shoes work, light bends, or the best way to cool down your hot cocoa, this chapter is for you. And if all you really want to do is smash a dozen eggs, there's an experiment in here just for you.

Marco Polo

In the game Marco Polo, a blindfolded player tries to locate his friends by listening to their yells. You have to be able to tell which direction sound is coming from if you want to win the game.

PROBLEM/PURPOSE

How does the distance sound travels affect how well can you tell which direction it comes from?

EXPERIMENT SUMMARY

You'll attempt to identify the direction sounds come from by tapping on a tube connecting your ears.

WHAT YOU NEED

▶ **Permanent marker**
▶ **Ruler**
▶ **4 feet (1.2 m) of rubber tube, ¼ inch (0.6 cm) in diameter***
▶ **Volunteers**
▶ **Pencil**

* The hardware store sells this as aquarium tubing.

EXPERIMENTAL PROCEDURE

1. Use the marker and ruler to mark and label 1-inch (2.5 cm) increments along the entire length of the tube.

2. Record the age and gender of your first volunteer. Have him hold one end of the tube to each ear so that the rest of the tube hangs across his back.

3. Use a pencil to tap one of the marks on the tube. Ask the volunteer which side (left, right, or couldn't tell) you were tapping on. Record the mark you tapped and his response.

4. Repeat step 3 for each of the marks on the tube. Tap the marks in a random order. Make sure you tap with the same force each time.

5. Repeat steps 2 through 4 for each of your volunteers.

CONCLUSION

Make a graph of the volunteers' responses for each of the marks on the tubes. Where were the volunteers able to identify correctly the direction of the sound? Where could they not tell which direction the sound came from? Was there any place where they thought the sound was coming from the wrong direction? Did you see any patterns related to gender or age?

TAKE A CLOSER LOOK

When you tap the tube, the sound travels through the tube in both directions. The ear closest to where you tap will receive the sound first. This is how the listener can tell which direction the sound comes from. For most people, there is a section of the tube about 4 inches (10.2 cm) long where they can't tell the direction of the sound. This is because sound takes $3/10,000$ of a second (or .0003 seconds) to travel 4 inches (10.2 cm) and the brain can't hear the difference in that small of an increment.

WHAT ELSE YOU CAN DO

Try this test with a longer or shorter tube. Compare the responses of young children to older adults. Does your perception of sound decrease with age? Do males and females hear differently? Try making different sounds, such as ringing a bell, at different positions around the room. Does distance matter when determining direction? Does the temperature of the room make a difference? Try this underwater in a swimming pool, where sound travels faster. What do you notice?

Boom! Boom!

Wax 'n' Tacks

 **Adult Supervision Required**

Have you ever noticed that pots and pans are made of different materials? Some are copper, some are steel, and others are aluminum. Do different pots and pans cook your food at different rates?

PROBLEM/PURPOSE

How do different types of metal affect the conduction of heat?

EXPERIMENT SUMMARY

You'll heat one end of a metal rod and use tacks attached with wax to measure the rate at which the heat moves along the rod.

WHAT YOU NEED

- Ruler
- Metal rods or thick wires in brass, aluminum, and copper*
- Permanent marker
- Lighter or matches
- Candle

- 6 to 10 metal thumbtacks
- Oven mitt
- Stopwatch

Each rod should be the same diameter and at least 1 foot (30.5 cm) long.

EXPERIMENTAL PROCEDURE

1. Using the ruler, measure and mark 1-inch (2.5 cm) intervals on the brass rod with the permanent marker.

2. Light the candle. Drip a little bit of melted wax onto the head of a thumbtack. Attach it to the rod at one of the marks. Attach tacks in this way along the length of the rod. Be careful.

3. Let the wax cool for 10 minutes.

4. Hold one end of the rod in the candle flame near the first tack. Use the oven mitt to protect your hand.

5. Use the stopwatch to time how long it takes all the tacks to fall off. Start the stopwatch when the first tack falls.

6. To calculate the rate the heat moved along the rod, or the heating speed, divide the number of inches (the number of tacks you attached minus 1) by the time it took them all to fall off.

7. Allow the brass rod to cool completely and repeat steps 2 through 6 five more times.

8. Repeat steps 1 through 7 using the aluminum and copper rods.

CONCLUSION

Which rod heated the fastest? Which heated the slowest? Make a graph of metal versus heating speed. Which material would make the best frying pan? Which would make the best cookie sheet? Is it always good to have pots and pans heat up quickly?

TAKE A CLOSER LOOK

When an object heats up, its atoms start moving, or vibrating, faster. In this case, heat is transferred along the metal rod through *conduction*. Conduction occurs as the atoms in the rod bounce around, causing the atoms near them to start moving as well. As the rod heats up, the atoms vibrate faster. If the atoms in a solid gain enough heat energy and start vibrating fast enough, the solid will melt and become a liquid.

Science Fair Math

Averages
During your science fair project, you should repeat each measurement several times to get rid of random error (see page 16). Since the numbers won't be the same every time, you'll need to calculate an *average* or *mean*. To do this, add all the numbers up and divide by total number of values you added. For example, if you measured the number of burnt popcorn kernels in four bags cooked in the microwave for 5 minutes to be 38, 24, 18, and 45, than the average would be calculated like this: $(38 + 24 + 18 + 45) \div 4 = 31$

This means that on average 31 burnt kernels were found in bags of popcorn cooked for five minutes.

Percentages
To show how much of a whole something is, you should calculate the percentage. To do this, divide the number by the amount of the whole and multiply by 100. For example, to find the percentage of burnt popcorn kernels in a bag of popcorn you would count the average number of burnt kernels (31) and the total number of kernels in the bag (523). $31 \div 523 \times 100 = 5.9$ percent. So about 6% of the popcorn kernels in the bag were burnt.

Metals in particular are good conductors because metal atoms have loose, free electrons that aren't attached to the metal atoms very well. Free electrons can easily jump from one atom to the other. This speeds up the transfer of heat energy between the atoms and causes metals to heat up faster.

WHAT ELSE YOU CAN DO

What other metals can you test? Does the thickness of the rod make a difference? How about the length? How could you test cooling rates?

Coin Toss

You and your best friend are debating who gets to eat the last chocolate chip cookie. You decide to use a coin so that "random chance" will determine who gets the treat. Is there a way to make sure you get the cookie without using a trick coin?

PROBLEM/PURPOSE

How does spinning a coin on its side affect whether it lands heads up or tails up?

EXPERIMENT SUMMARY

You'll spin different coins on their sides several times each to determine the percentage of heads-up and tails-up landings.

WHAT YOU NEED

- ▶ **5 pennies**
- ▶ **5 nickels**
- ▶ **5 dimes**
- ▶ **5 quarters**
- ▶ **Dish soap**
- ▶ **Hot water**
- ▶ **Toothbrush**
- ▶ **Cloth**
- ▶ **Smooth tabletop**

EXPERIMENTAL PROCEDURE

1. Soak the coins in hot, soapy water for 30 minutes. Scrub them with a toothbrush for several minutes, then dry them with a cloth. You want to make sure that the type of coin and not its accumulated dirt determines your results.

2. Hold one penny so that its edge is on the table. Quickly flick the penny so it spins like a top. (This may take some practice.)

3. Record whether the penny lands heads or tails up. Be sure to record only results for spins where the penny rotates like a top.

4. Give each penny 20 good spins and record how they land each time. Using five different pennies will keep any defects in the penny from affecting your results.

5. Because you've spun the pennies 100 times, the number of times the coin landed heads up is equal to the percentage of times the coin lands heads up. The number of times the coin landed tails up is the percentage of times the coin lands tails up.

6. Repeat steps 2 through 4 for each of the other coins.

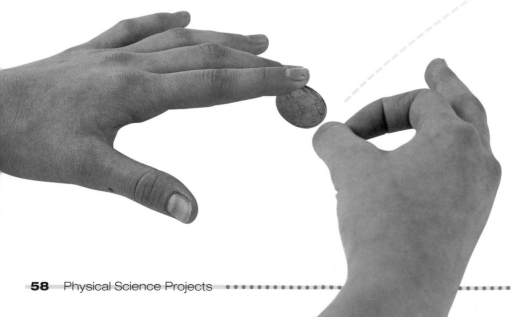

CONCLUSION

Make a bar graph of the type of coin and the percentage of times it lands heads up. Is this more or less than 50 percent? Which coin would you choose to spin when making a bet? Why do you think the coins act differently?

TAKE A CLOSER LOOK

Due to the designs on the surfaces of the coins, one side is usually heavier than the other. The coin is pulled down onto the heavy side more often than the lighter side. When you toss a coin in the air, there are many other factors, such as the height, speed, and angle at which you throw the coin, that affect the side the coin lands on. These factors cancel out the effects of the coin's slight imbalance.

WHAT ELSE YOU CAN DO

How else can you manipulate a coin to land on different sides? Look around the house for coins from other countries. Can you predict how they will land before trying the experiment? Try timing how long each coin spins to see whether the spin time affects which side it will land on.

Helpful Hint

If you spin the penny more or less than 100 times you can calculate the percentage using the following formula:

(# of times the coin landed heads up) ÷ (Total number of spins) x 100 = percentage the coin lands heads up

Down the Drain

You've probably heard the old saying that toilets flush the opposite way in the Southern Hemisphere, and you've probably wondered what would happen if you flushed a toilet at the equator. But have you ever wondered if the old saying is really true?

PROBLEM/PURPOSE

How does the Coriolis force affect the way water drains on the Northern and Southern Hemispheres?

EXPERIMENT SUMMARY

You'll carefully drain sinks and flush toilets to see whether the water always drains the same way in the hemisphere you live in.

WHAT YOU NEED

▸ **Sinks**
▸ **Toilets**

EXPERIMENTAL PROCEDURE

1. Fill the sink halfway with water. Turn the water off completely and wait at least 5 minutes so that the water is completely still. Make sure no one walks near the sink or disturbs the water in any way. You want to be sure that the direction in which the water drains is not due to other forces.

2. Slowly and carefully remove the plug and watch the water drain down the sink. Record the direction in which the water spins. Note whether the direction changes while the water drains.

3. Repeat steps 1 and 2, testing the same sink at least three more times.

4. Find a clean toilet and, just as you did with the sink, make sure the water is very still. Flush the toilet. Record the direction in which the water spins. Also, note whether water pouring back into the toilet affects the direction in which the water drains.

5. Test the same toilet at least three more times.

6. Test as many sinks and toilets as you can.

CONCLUSION

Make a bar graph for sinks and toilets and the direction in which the water drained. Did the water always drain the same way? What factors do you think might affect the direction in which water drains?

The *Coriolis force* is caused by the rotation of the Earth. Everything on the planet rotates with the Earth. If you were able to look down on the North Pole of the spinning Earth, you would see that it turns counterclockwise. If you then look at the South Pole, you would see it spins clockwise. Check this out on a globe!

But because the Earth rotates relatively slowly—about once every day—this force is extremely small. For very large amounts of slow-moving fluids, such as the atmosphere, it has a larger, lasting effect. Hurricanes in the Northern Hemisphere spin counterclockwise and in the Southern Hemisphere they spin clockwise—just like the Earth. Also like the Earth, hurricanes turn relatively slowly and the direction of the spin is controlled by the direction in which the Earth spins.

For smaller amounts of a fluid, such as the water in your sink, this force is strongly outweighed by even the tiniest disturbances and design flaws in the sink. These factors are more likely to influence the direction in which the water drains than the Coriolis force does.

Where are You?

Suppose you get captured by space aliens (hey, it could happen!) and dropped in some unknown location. How could you figure out if you were in the Northern or Southern Hemisphere? You could rush to the nearest toilet and give it a flush. But if you think that's going to work, go back and do the "Down the Drain" project. Besides walking up to the nearest person and asking, how could you figure out where you are?

1 What is the season?
Is it snowing in July? Are you melting in the middle of December? Then you're probably in the Southern Hemisphere. When it's summer in the Northern Hemisphere, the top part of the Earth (North) is tilted towards the sun, which means the suns rays are more direct, the weather is warmer, and days are longer. Of course, this means the other half of the earth (the Southern Hemisphere) is tilted away, and those indirect sun rays mean winter.

2 Head south.
Take a trip south and see what happens. If you see lots of snow and penguins then you've made it to Antarctica and you're in the Southern Hemisphere. If you see monkeys and tropical rainforests then welcome to the equator! You're In the Northern Hemisphere.

3 Look for a tornado.
While the affect of the Earth's rotation (Coriolis effect) on such small systems as sinks and toilets is dubious, its affect on large systems like hurricanes and tornadoes is undeniable. If you see a tornado, first head for cover, and then see if you can tell which way it's spinning. In the Northern Hemisphere tornadoes and hurricanes rotate counter-clockwise. In the Southern Hemisphere, they spin clockwise.

4 Plug in your computer.
If the space aliens were kind enough to let you bring your computer (with a cathode ray tube monitor of course) you can simply take a look at the screen to tell what hemisphere you're on. CRT monitors (the big bulky ones, not the nice flat LCD panels) and some TVs work by shooting electrons across the screen. The Earth has its own magnetic field that depends on which hemisphere you're in. (Where do you think the north and south poles on magnets came from?) This magnetic field affects the electrons shooting across your screen. If you try to use a Northern Hemisphere monitor in the Southern Hemisphere you would notice that the color and picture are distorted.

The Amazing Floating Paper Clip

Magnetism and gravity are two forces that act without contact. If you hold a ball up in the air, it's not touching the Earth but the Earth's gravity still pulls it down. How can you affect these invisible forces?

PROBLEM/PURPOSE

How do different materials affect the flow of magnetic force?

EXPERIMENT SUMMARY

You'll use a strong magnet to suspend a paper clip in midair and use materials to try to block the magnetic force.

WHAT YOU NEED

▸ **Strong magnet***
▸ **Screwdriver**
▸ **Tall glass**
▸ **1-foot (30.5 cm) length of thread**
▸ **Paper clip**
▸ **Tape**
▸ **Tabletop**
▸ **Potential magnetic-force-blocking materials: penny, paper, cloth, styrofoam plate, plastic plate, craft stick, eraser, key**

* Available at hardware stores

EXPERIMENTAL PROCEDURE

1. Place the magnet on the end of the screwdriver. Balance the screwdriver on top of the glass so the magnet hangs out about 3 inches (7.6 cm) from the edge of the glass.

2. Tie the thread to the paper clip and stick it to the magnet.

3. Loosely tape the thread to the tabletop. Begin pulling the thread slowly through the tape until you pull the paper clip off the magnet and it floats ½ to 1 inch (1.3 to 2.5 cm) from the magnet. The paper clip is caught between the upward force from the magnet and the downward force from the thread and gravity. Press the tape down firmly so the paper clip stays put. Now you can test which materials can block the magnetic field.

4. Carefully hold the penny between the paper clip and the magnet. Be very careful not to touch the paper clip. Observe and record any change in the position of the paper clip.

5. Repeat step 4 with the rest of the test materials.

CONCLUSION

Which materials had no effect on the position of the paper clip? What materials completely blocked the magnetic force, making the paper clip fall to the table? Did any materials block only some of the magnetic force? Did any materials make it stronger?

WHAT ELSE YOU CAN DO

What other materials can you test? Does the size of the magnet or paper clip matter? What happens if the paper clip is closer or further from the magnet? Try layering the materials. For example, use two pennies or ten pieces of paper instead of just one.

TAKE A CLOSER LOOK

Magnetic forces are caused when the electrons spinning around the atoms in the magnet line up. This means that all the electrons are spinning around the atoms in the same direction. When the paper clip touches the magnet, it becomes magnetized, so the electrons spinning around the paper clip's atoms line up. The force between the magnet and the paper clip keep it magnetized. This happens more easily in some materials such as iron, nickel, and cobalt than it does in other materials such as plastic, water, and wood. However, if you place another easily magnetized material between the magnet and the paper clip, the new object becomes magnetized and blocks the force holding up the paper clip.

Charged Up

Have you ever been walking around the house and, when you grab a metal doorknob, you get a shock? Which materials produce the biggest zap?

PROBLEM/PURPOSE

Which materials generate the best electrical charge?

EXPERIMENT SUMMARY

You'll rub a variety of materials against a balloon to see which generates the greatest electrical charge.

WHAT YOU NEED

- ►Hole punch
- ►Construction paper
- ►Ruler
- ►Tabletop
- ►Masking tape
- ►Helium-quality balloons
- ►Stopwatch
- ►Lighter or matches
- ►Candle
- ►Rubbing materials:

    Wool sock, nylon panty hose, silk tie (or piece of silk cloth), piece of plastic wrap 10 inches (25.4 cm) square, sheet of paper, styrofoam plate, glass plate, unfinished piece of wood, hair (the stuff on your head works great), cotton sock

Ha ha ha. . .
I rule static electricity!

Ouch!

EXPERIMENTAL PROCEDURE

1. Use the hole punch to punch holes in the construction paper. Collect 100 of the paper dots and, using a ruler, spread them evenly on the tabletop in a 6-inch (15.2 cm) square. Use the masking tape to mark the boundaries of the square.

2. Blow up a balloon and rub it with the wool sock for 10 seconds. Use the stopwatch to time yourself.

3. Hold the balloon 1 inch (2.5 cm) above the center of the dots until the dots stop jumping onto the balloon.

4. Quickly move the balloon to a clear area and count the number of dots that were attracted to the balloon. (Be sure to include those that fell off after you moved the balloon away from the pile of dots.) Record the number of dots.

5. Remove all the paper dots from the balloon and put them back inside the 6-inch square. Light the candle and carefully wave the balloon about 1 foot (30.5 cm) over it for a few seconds. The ions produced by the burning candle will get rid of the static charge on the balloon.

6. Test the wool sock five more times and calculate the average number of dots attracted by the balloon. Record the average and any other observations you made.

7. Repeat steps 2 through 6 for all the rubbing materials, using a new balloon for each material.

CONCLUSION

Average the number of dots each rubbing material attracted. Make a bar graph of the number of dots attracted to the balloon for each rubbing material. Which materials caused the balloon to attract the most dots? Which caused the balloon to attract the fewest? What relationship do you see between these materials?

TAKE A CLOSER LOOK

Most materials are either a conductor or an insulator. *Conductors* allow electrical charges to flow through them. *Insulators* prevent the flow of electrical charges. When you rub two insulators together, such as wool and a latex balloon, electrons are pulled from one material and deposited on the other. For example, electrons are pulled from the wool and deposited on the balloon. The balloon becomes negatively charged because it holds onto more negatively charged electrons than the wool sock does. When you walk on a wool carpet with leather-soled shoes, the wool carpet pulls electrons off the leather, causing you to become positively charged. When you touch the metal doorknob, a conductor, the electrons flow onto your body, causing a shock.

WHAT ELSE YOU CAN DO

What other materials could you test? Try rubbing the materials suggested above on a glass plate instead of a balloon. How are your results different? Does human fur (hair), dog fur, or cat fur work better for charging balloons?

In this experiment, the number of paper dots attracted by the balloon measured how much charge was built up on the balloon. When the balloon is discharged or the charge jumps off onto something else, such as your hand, sometimes a spark occurs. Which material would you use to make the biggest spark? Test it out by rolling up a piece of aluminum foil into a small lightning rod (about the size of a small pencil). Hold it close to a charged balloon. If you don't see a spark, you should at least hear the hissing sound of the balloon discharging to the foil. (Lightning rods are large metal spikes put on top of houses. They drain the electric charge out of the sky in order to prevent lightning strikes.)

"Hot Cocoa, Anyone?"

You've just made a cup of hot cocoa. You know that adding milk would make it creamier, but you don't want your cocoa to get cold. What should you do? This is a great project for a cold winter day.

PROBLEM/PURPOSE

How does the time at which you add milk to hot cocoa affect its temperature?

EXPERIMENT SUMMARY

You'll add cold water to boiling water at different times to see how the cold water affects the temperature of the boiling water.

WHAT YOU NEED

- ▶ Measuring cup
- ▶ Water
- ▶ Pitcher
- ▶ Refrigerator
- ▶ Stopwatch
- ▶ Thermometer
- ▶ Teakettle
- ▶ Stove
- ▶ Styrofoam cups

EXPERIMENTAL PROCEDURE

1. Pour about 3 cups of water into the pitcher and place it in the refrigerator. This will represent the milk. Start the stopwatch. After the pitcher has cooled for about 30 minutes, use the thermometer to measure and record the temperature of the water.

2. Put another 3 cups (.7 l) of water into the teakettle and bring it to a boil on the stove.

3. Carefully pour ½ cup (137.8 ml) of boiling water into a styrofoam cup. Use the thermometer to measure and record the starting temperature of the water.

4. Immediately pour in ½ cup (137.8 ml) of cold water from the pitcher. Again, measure and record the temperature of the mixed water. It might take a few seconds for the temperature to stabilize.

5. Repeat steps 2 through 4, waiting 2 minutes before adding the cold water. Be sure to reboil the water and put the pitcher back in the fridge each time. Continue increasing the length of time before adding the cold water to the boiling water. Repeat steps 2 through 4 for 4, 6, 8, and 10 minutes.

6. Calculate the temperature change for each of the trials by subtracting the temperature of the mixed water from the temperature of the hot water.

CONCLUSION

Make a graph of time before adding the cold water versus the final temperature of the mixed water. What patterns do you see? Will the cocoa stay hottest if you add the milk immediately or wait? Why do you think this is?

TAKE A CLOSER LOOK

It makes sense that a big pot of hot water will cool a lot slower than a small cup. In general, large things change temperature a lot slower than small things because there are more molecules to cool down or heat up. The same applies to your hot cocoa. If you add the milk right away, you've doubled the amount of liquid and the hot cocoa will cool down slower. If you wait, the hot cocoa will cool down still further before you add the milk. So, when to add the milk depends on how hot you want your drink.

WHAT ELSE YOU CAN DO

Try using real hot cocoa and milk to redo the experiment. Does water make a good substitute? Try the experiment using a ceramic mug instead of a styrofoam cup. Does the container make a difference? Bring some friends over and have them taste the cocoa at different temperatures. What is the ideal temperature for drinking hot cocoa? Be careful not to burn your tongue!

Science Sayings Quiz

You've probably heard the saying "A watched pot never boils" but have you ever heard: "A vessel under optical supervision never reaches a temperature of 212 Fahrenheit?"

Take a break from your science fair project, pull out a dictionary, and match each saying with its "scientificated" version.

Sayings

1. Birds of a feather flock together.
2. A stitch in time saves nine.
3. Haste makes waste.
4. A bird in the hand is worth two in the bush.
5. Curiosity killed the cat.
6. A dog is man's best friend.
7. All's fair in love and war.
8. You can't squeeze blood from a turnip.
9. Every cloud has a silver lining.
10. Never look a gift horse in the mouth.
11. A fool and his money are soon parted.

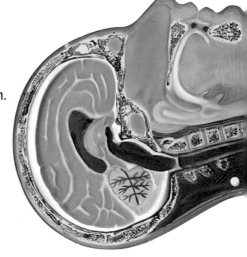

Scientificated Sayings

A. The inquisitiveness of a member of the feline species was responsible for its extinction.

B. Each cumulus formation is possessed of an inner surface covering made of argentums.

C. Accelerated execution produces faulty results.

D. An individual with poor judgment and his collateral are soon estranged.

E. Plumaged birds of the same species congregate in the same area.

F. You can get away with anything in dealing with Eros and Ares.

G. One feathered aerial biped imprisoned digitally is equal in value to twice that many aboreally located.

H. Never subject a presented equine to denticular inspection.

I. A carnivorous mammal of the family Candidae is the genus Homo's most loyal compeer.

J. It's impossible to extract a plasma in which corpuscles are suspended from the edible root of a certain brassicaceous plant.

K. A polished steel instrument used at the appropriate moment will be tantamount to the saving of three times three.

Go Fly a Kite

The sun is shining and the wind is blowing strong. It looks like the perfect day to fly a kite. But how do you know whether the wind is just right?

SAFETY: *Don't fly your kite in areas where there are power lines, transmission towers, or trees. Don't fly your kite during a thunderstorm.*

PROBLEM/PURPOSE

How does wind speed affect the stability of a kite?

EXPERIMENT SUMMARY

You'll build a simple kite and fly it in a variety of wind speeds.

WHAT YOU NEED

▶ **Kite (see page 69)**
▶ **Access to the Internet or TV**
▶ **Helper**
▶ **Stopwatch**

EXPERIMENTAL PROCEDURE

1. Make the kite on page 69. Record the local wind speed. You can find this on the local news or online at www.weather.com.

2. Find a safe area to fly the kite.

3. Have your helper use the stopwatch to time the number of seconds it takes to get the kite into the air. Record the time.

4. When the kite is in the air, determine the stability of the kite using the scale on page 69.

5. Record the stability level.

6. Repeat steps 1 through 5 on five days that have different wind speeds.

CONCLUSION

How much time was required to get your kite in the air? How did this time vary with wind speed? Make a graph of wind speed versus the time to get the kite in the air.

How stable was your kite in the different wind speeds? Make a graph of wind speed versus stability. Would you expect your kite to have more or less stability on an extremely windy day?

How would you design your kite differently?

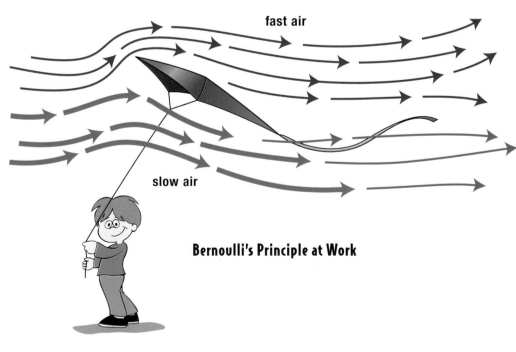

fast air

slow air

Bernoulli's Principle at Work

TAKE A CLOSER LOOK

What makes a kite fly in the first place? Air pressure, which is the force of the air molecules pushing on the kite, makes the kite fly. In the 1600s, an Italian scientist named Daniel Bernoulli figured out how pressure and gasses work. He summed it up in a theory called *Bernoulli's Principle*. Bernoulli said that fast-moving air has a lower pressure, or force, than slow-moving air. As you pull the kite through the air, the air that goes over the top of the kite has further to go. It has to move faster than the air beneath the kite. So the air on top of the kite has less pressure than the slower-moving air beneath the kite. Therefore the stronger pressure beneath the kite pushes it upward. The string keeps the kite tilted so that you get maximum lift, or upward force.

WHAT ELSE YOU CAN DO

Try different kite designs and see how their stability varies in different wind speeds. How would a tail affect the stability of your kite? How about the materials used to make your kite? Does the length of string you let out for your kite (in other words, the height at which your kite flies) affect the stability?

Building a Kite

WHAT YOU NEED

- ▶ **2 balsa wood dowels, ¼ inch (0.6 cm) in diameter**
- ▶ **Saw**
- ▶ **Scissors**
- ▶ **Kite string**
- ▶ **Glue or paste**
- ▶ **Crepe paper**

WHAT YOU DO

1. Cut the balsa wood dowels with the saw so that one piece is 26 inches (66 cm) long and the other is 22 inches (55.9 cm) long.

2. Use scissors to make notches about ½ inch (1.3 cm) from each end of the wood sticks.

3. Place the shorter piece so that it is centered 7 inches (17.8 cm) from the top of the longer piece, creating a cross shape (see figure).

4. Wrap a length of string around the intersection of the two sticks in an X to hold the two sticks together. Tie a knot in the ends. You may use some glue as well if you want.

5. Tie string around the ends of each stick in the notches so that it makes a diamond shape (see figure 2). The string should be taut, but not so tight that it bends the sticks.

6. Cut out a piece of crepe paper in a diamond shape 2 inches (5.1 cm) bigger than your kite. The paper should be 28 inches (71.1 cm) tall and 24 inches (61 cm) wide.

7. Lay your wood and string frame over the crepe paper. Spread the glue or paste along the edges of the paper.

8. Carefully fold the paper over the string and press it together firmly. Be careful not to tear the paper.

9. Once the glue has dried, tie the end of your kite string to the intersection of the two sticks. This is the string you will use to fly your kite.

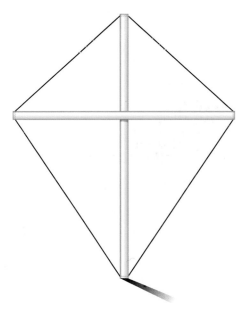

Kite Stability Scale

5 is the most stable and 1 is the least stable:

5 Kite remains stable in an upright position.

4 Kite remains upright but moves about.

3 Kite moves about at regular intervals, dips, and twists.

2 Kite does complete revolution approximately every 15 to 20 seconds.

1 Kite is constantly rotating.

Light It Up

Adult Supervision Required

Thomas Edison's bright idea about how to make the lightbulb work wasn't the result of a sudden flash of inspiration. He tried hundreds of times to make *filaments* that would glow and not burn up, and he used many different materials, from cardboard to bamboo, for his filaments. (The filament is the part of the lightbulb that glows when the electricity heats it.) How well will different thicknesses of iron wire work as a filament?

PROBLEM/PURPOSE

How does the thickness of an iron filament affect how long it will glow?

EXPERIMENT SUMMARY

You'll make a lightbulb and test filaments to find which gives the longest lasting lightbulb.

WHAT YOU NEED

► **Wire cutters**
► **3 feet (91.4 cm) of shielded copper wire***
► **Wire strippers (optional)**
► **1-inch (2.5 cm) nail**
► **Cork stopper for a lid**
► **Pencil**
► **Picture hanging wire**
► **Small jar**
► **6-volt battery**
► **Electrical tape**
► **Stopwatch**

* Available at hardware stores

EXPERIMENTAL PROCEDURE

1. Use the wire cutters to cut the copper wire into two pieces, each about 1½ feet (45.7 cm) long. Cut off 1 inch (2.5 cm) of the plastic coating at each end of the strands using the wire cutters. Cut through the plastic and pull it off the wire. (You can use wire strippers if you have a pair.)

2. With a nail, make two holes that pass through the cork from top to bottom. Push the stripped ends of each piece of wire through one of the holes so that you can see about 2 inches (5.1 cm) of each on the other side.

3. Wrap the ends of the wire halfway around the pencil to make hooks at the ends of the copper wires. You'll twist small strands of iron wire around these hooks to make a filament.

4. Unwind the picture hanging wire so that you can use the individual fine strands of iron wire.

5. Twist two strands of the iron wire together. Stretch the strands of iron wire across the gap between the two copper hooks to form the filament. Twist each end of the strand around the copper hooks to hold it in place.

6. Put the cork stopper with the filament inside the jar.

7. Carefully hook up both copper wire ends to the battery, using a small piece of the electrical tape to attach one to the positive end and the other to the negative end of the battery. Watch your bulb light up and start the stopwatch.

8. Time how long your filament glows. When the filament stops glowing, record the time. Unhook the ends of the wire from the battery. Wait 2 minutes before pulling the cork out of the jar. Remove the filament, let it cool, and then throw it away. Be careful. The filament gets very hot!

9. Repeat steps 5 through 8 using two strands of wire for a filament twice more. Calculate the average length of time the bulb glowed.

10. Repeat steps 5 through 9, adding a wire strand each time.

CONCLUSION

Which filament made the longest lasting lightbulb? Make a graph of the number of iron wire strands you used for the filament versus the time the lightbulb burned. Which filament gave the brightest light? What problems did you have getting your lightbulb to burn? Is this a practical way to light your home?

TAKE A CLOSER LOOK

The idea of the lightbulb has been around for quite a while, although Edison is often credited with inventing it. Through trial and error, he was able to find the right material (carbon) and the right thickness to make a long-lasting bulb. (This experiment uses iron because it's easy to work with.)

The electric lightbulb works because you have made a complete circuit with electrical current flowing out from the battery, through the filament, and back to the battery. Electrical current is the flow of electrons, usually from the positive terminal of the battery to the negative terminal. The electricity flowing through the wire produces heat and makes the filament glow. Different types of materials and different thicknesses will act differently.

WHAT ELSE YOU CAN DO

Try other materials for your filament, such as copper wire or brass wire. Can you make a bamboo or cardboard filament like Edison did? (Be very careful, because this is a fire hazard. Make sure an adult is supervising.) How could you measure the brightness of your lightbulb?

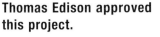

Thomas Edison approved this project.

Slip & Slide

Have you ever watched a basketball game and heard the squeak of shoes on the floor? This is caused by players using the friction of their shoes against the floor to stop. *Friction* is a force that occurs when two surfaces slide across each other.

How does weight affect the friction of shoes?

squeek!
eeek!
ook!

EXPERIMENT SUMMARY

You'll measure the friction of your shoes on the floor as you increase the weight in the shoes.

WHAT YOU NEED

- ▶ **Pair of shoes (basketball shoes or sneakers work best)**
- ▶ **Scale**
- ▶ **12-inch-long (30.5 cm) piece of string**
- ▶ **Spring scale***
- ▶ **Tape**
- ▶ **Yardstick**
- ▶ **Floor with about 3 feet (91.4 cm) of clear space**
- ▶ **Stopwatch**
- ▶ **Helper**
- ▶ **Canned food, small bag of sand, or small rocks**

* You can borrow a spring scale from your science teacher or get one from a science store.

EXPERIMENTAL PROCEDURE

1. Put one of the shoes on the scale and record its weight.

2. Tie one end of the string to the shoelaces, closest to the toe of the shoe. You should be able to drag the shoe slowly so that the entire bottom of the shoe stays in contact with the floor.

3. Make a loop in the other end of the string and attach it to the hook at the bottom of the spring scale.

4. Use the tape and yardstick to mark a 3-foot-long (91.4 cm) space on the floor. You'll need to pull the shoe at a constant speed to make this experiment work correctly. With the stopwatch, time how long it takes for you to drag the shoe from start to finish. Record the time it takes for you to pull the shoe 3 feet. To determine the speed at which you're pulling the shoe, divide the distance (3 feet [91.4 cm]) by the time it takes you to pull the shoe.

5. Practice dragging your shoe by the end of the spring scale across the floor. Keep the spring scale and string as parallel as possible to the floor. Have your helper use the stopwatch to make sure that you're pulling the shoe at a constant speed.

6. Once you're comfortable pulling the shoe at a constant speed, observe the force reading on the spring scale. When the shoe is moving, the reading should change very little. Record the value in pounds, ounces, or Newtons, depending on the scale you are using. (These are all just different units of force, like the way Celsius and Fahrenheit are different units for measuring temperature.)

7. Repeat step 6 at least five more times.

8. Calculate and record the average force needed to pull the shoe. This is the friction force for your shoe on the floor.

9. Add some weight to the shoe. You can use a can of soup, a small bag of sand, or some rocks to make the shoe heavier. Place the heavier shoe on the scale and record the new weight.

10. Repeat steps 6 through 8 for the new shoe weight. Make sure you're pulling the shoe at the same speed.

11. Add weight to your shoe three more times, so that you have a total of five different weights. Place the shoe on the scale and record its weight each time you change it. Repeat steps 6 through 8 for each shoe weight.

CONCLUSION

Calculate the coefficient of friction for each shoe weight. To do this, divide the friction force you recorded in step 8 by the weight of the shoe. Make a graph of coefficient of friction versus shoe weight. Do you see any patterns? Did the coefficient of friction change with weight? What problems did you have measuring the force of friction?

TAKE A CLOSER LOOK

The *coefficient of friction* is just a number that describes the friction between two surfaces, regardless of weight. This number should be about the same for each shoe weight. The coefficient of friction for rubber (like your shoe soles) on

linoleum (like most kitchen floors) is generally 0.5 to 0.8. Your coefficient of friction should be somewhere around these numbers depending on the type of shoe and floor you used. As you increase the weight of your shoe, the force needed to pull the shoe also increases, so the ratio of the two (the coefficient of friction) stays the same.

Similarly, if you change the surface area by dragging two shoes next to each other, the coefficient of friction stays the same. The amount of area in which the shoes touch the floor increases but the weight pushing down on that area is more spread out.

WHAT ELSE YOU CAN DO

Does the direction in which you pull the shoes matter? What about the surface area? Try pulling two shoes together, side by side, and then pull one on top of the other to check out the effect of surface area. The shoes will have the same weight; do they have the same friction force? Try different types of shoes and different types of surfaces. Try sports shoes such as tennis shoes, bowling shoes, basketball shoes, or even dancing shoes on the surfaces they are used on. Does the amount of friction you find make sense for the sport they are used in? What if you drag the shoes on different types of floors?

Supersonic

An airplane or a car is said to be *supersonic* if it travels faster than the speed of sound. But does sound always travel at the same speed?

PROBLEM/PURPOSE

How does temperature affect the speed of sound?

EXPERIMENT SUMMARY

You'll use a metal pipe and a metronome to measure the speed of sound on warm and cold days.

WHAT YOU NEED

- ▶ **Large building**
- ▶ **Metal pipe**
- ▶ **Hammer**
- ▶ **Helper**
- ▶ **Metronome***
- ▶ **Measuring Tape**
- ▶ **Thermometer**

* You can get a metronome from a music store, or a music teacher might let you borrow one.

EXPERIMENTAL PROCEDURE

1. Find a large building such as a school that you can stand 80 to 100 yards (73.2 to 91.4 m) away (about the length of a football field) from and hear the echo when you bang on the metal pipe with your hammer. Bring along your helper and the metronome.

2. Begin tapping very steadily and slowly on the pipe. Gradually increase the time between taps so that you tap on the pipe at the exact same time that the echo is heard. (When this happens you won't hear the echo because you are tapping at the same time.)

3. Have your helper use the metronome to measure the frequency (the rate) of the tapping. Turn on the metronome and adjust the frequency so that the metronome is ticking at the same rate as you are tapping. Record this frequency from the metronome in beats per minute.

4. Use the measuring tape to measure and record the distance between you and the building.

5. Measure and record the temperature of the air with the thermometer.

6. Calculate the time it took the sound to travel to the wall and back in seconds by dividing 60 seconds by the frequency in beats per minute.

7. Calculate the distance the sound traveled to the wall and back by multiplying your distance to the wall by two.

8. Calculate the speed of the sound by dividing the distance the sound traveled (from step 7) by the time it took to go that far (from step 6).

9. Repeat steps 2 through 8 at different air temperatures. Try collecting data in the morning or evening, when it is cooler, and in the late afternoon, when it is warmest.

CONCLUSION

Make a graph of temperature versus speed of sound. What patterns do you see? Why do you think sound might travel different speeds at different temperatures? What problems did you have collecting data?

TAKE A CLOSER LOOK

The speed of sound depends on the density of the material it travels through. Vibrations in the material, such as air, transmit sound. One molecule starts vibrating and bumps into another molecule, which starts vibrating and bumps into another molecule. The closer the molecules are together, the faster they bump into each other and the faster the sound travels. Because cool air is denser than hot air, the air molecules are closer together, so sound travels faster in cool air.

Sound also travels much more slowly than light does. This is why you see lightning before you hear the thunder. Sound travels very slowly in air. Cowboys and farmers on the prairie would put their ears to the rails to hear whether a train was coming because the sound traveled more quickly through the metal rails than it did through the air.

WHAT ELSE YOU CAN DO

Test other factors that might affect the speed of sound, such as humidity and altitude. Can you think of another way to measure the time and distance sound travels to calculate its speed? Convert your speeds to miles per hour. Could a car travel that fast?

Science Fair Vocabulary

Wow your friends and family, as well as the judges, with your use of these technical science fair terms!

Apparatus: The tools you use to perform your experiment.

Controls: All the other variables that could affect the outcome of your experiment that you try to keep constant. For example, the brand of popcorn, the type of microwave, and the temperature at which you store the popcorn is kept the same each time you perform the experiment.

Dependent Variable: The variable that depends on what you do to the independent variable. For example, the number of unburnt kernels depends on the amount of time the popcorn spends in the microwave.

Hypothesis: An educated guess about whether two variables are related.

Independent Variable: The variable that you manipulate. For example, you can change the amount of time the popcorn is in the microwave.

Prediction: What you think might happen in your experiment or how the two variables in your hypothesis are related.

Qualitative values: Anything that can't be measured such as color, texture, or month of the year.

Quantitative values: Anything that can be measured. For instance, you can measure the number of popcorn kernels or time in the microwave.

Subject: Either topic of your project or the people, animals, or things you're experimenting on.

Variable: The values that you are working with in your experiment, both qualitative and quantitative.

Upside-Down Toast

You're just about to bite into a yummy piece of toast when it slips out of your hands. Before it even lands you know it's going to end up butter-side down. Is this a universal law of physics or just bad luck?

PROBLEM/PURPOSE

How does distance affect whether toast lands land butter-side up or down?

EXPERIMENT SUMMARY

You'll drop toast from different heights to see whether distance affects the side your toast lands on.

WHAT YOU NEED

▶ **Toaster**
▶ **Sliced bread**
▶ **Aluminum foil or plastic wrap**
▶ **Yardstick**
▶ **Low table (less than 26 inches [66 cm] high)**
▶ **Books**

EXPERIMENTAL PROCEDURE

1. Toast a slice of bread. Use the aluminum foil or plastic wrap to wrap one side of the toast. The wrap simulates the weight of butter and keeps your toast from falling apart after you drop it a few times. (And you won't have to clean butter off the floor when you're done with the experiment.)

2. Measure and record the height of your table.

3. Place your toast near the edge of the table. Pushing on the back edge, slowly slide it until it starts to fall off the table.

4. Record whether your toast lands butter-side up or down. (The wrapped side is the buttered side.) Also note whether your toast lands on one of its edges and then flips over.

5. Repeat steps 3 and 4 at least 10 times. Make sure you push the toast off the table at the same speed each time.

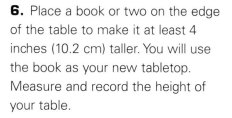

6. Place a book or two on the edge of the table to make it at least 4 inches (10.2 cm) taller. You will use the book as your new tabletop. Measure and record the height of your table.

7. Repeat steps 2 through 5, dropping the toast from this new height.

8. Repeat steps 6 and 7, making another tabletop 4 inches (10.2 cm) higher than the last one. Continue dropping toast from different height tabletops until you reach at least 48 inches (121.9 cm). Replace the toast when it's battered from dropping it so much.

CONCLUSION

Make a chart that compares the butter-side down and butter-side up landings for the different table heights. From which height did your toast land butter-side down the most? From which height did your toast land butter-side up the most? Why do you think the toast landed on its edge at some heights and not others?

TAKE A CLOSER LOOK

As the toast slides off the edge of the table, the leading edge starts to rotate downward, making the toast spin as it falls through the air. If the table is high enough, the toast will make a complete rotation so that it lands butter-side up. If the table is too low, there won't be enough time for the toast to spin all the way around, so it will land butter-side down.

WHAT ELSE YOU CAN DO

What difference would a heavier spread, such as peanut butter and jelly, make? How about no spread at all? Does the size of the toast matter? How about the surface it lands on? Would your results vary if you pushed the toast off quickly rather than sliding it gently?

Land on Your Feet

Why is it that your toast will land butter side down but cats always land on their feet? And which side would a buttered cat land on? (Just kidding.)

When a cat falls upside down many things happen in the fraction of a second it takes to fall. First, the head turns until it is facing down. Then the front legs are brought up to his face and the front part of the body is brought in line with the head. Next, the back legs are brought in and the cat twists its rear half to catch up with the front. As he is about to land, the cat stretches all four legs out and arches his back to reduce the impact force on his body when he hits the ground. The cat's tail stiffens and rotates the whole time, acting as a counterbalance. That is, by rotating in the opposite direction as the rest of the cat, the tail balances out his turning motion.

While this seems incredibly complicated, cats do it automatically. Scientists call it the *righting reflex*. If you ask a physicist, she will say the cat conserves *angular momentum* as it falls. Angular momentum is an object's (or cat's) tendency to keep rotating, and it depends on the direction and how fast the cat is rotating, as well as how far out it stretches. Like a spinning ice skater, the cat uses his front and rear legs to control how fast and which way the different parts of his body turn.

If a cat falls a short distance, he can usually flip himself over and land on his feet. If he falls more than one or two floors, however, he might get hurt by the impact of the fall. Because they are light and furry, cats reach *terminal velocity* after falling only five stories or so. Terminal velocity is the point where air resistance prevents you from speeding up any more as you fall. For cats, terminal velocity is about 60 miles per hour. Although a cat can flip himself around, his legs and feet cannot absorb the shock at this speed.

* This experiment is NOT appropriate for your science fair project OR your cat. Use the toast instead.

Making Waves

When you jump rope, you're actually jumping over a wave. The turners on each side of the rope are turning together so that the rope makes a smooth arc. This is half of a *standing wave*. A standing wave is a vibration that fits exactly on a length of string and therefore appears not to move.

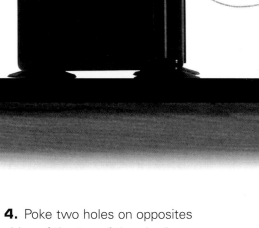

PROBLEM/PURPOSE

How does tension affect your ability to make multiple standing waves?

EXPERIMENT SUMMARY

You'll add different amounts of weight to the end of a vibrating string to form standing waves.

WHAT YOU NEED

▶ **Screwdriver**
▶ **Basic aquarium pump***
▶ **4-foot (121.9 cm) and 1-foot (30.5 cm) lengths of string**
▶ **Countertop or table**
▶ **2 C-clamps****
▶ **Large plastic cup**
▶ **Scissors**
▶ **Spoon**
▶ **Bucket of sand**
▶ **Scale**

* Available at pet stores

** Available at hardware and home improvement stores

EXPERIMENTAL PROCEDURE

1. Use the screwdriver to carefully remove the plastic housing on the aquarium pump. Make sure the pump is unplugged when you do this. The pump will make the string vibrate, just like the turners in jump rope.

2. Plug in the pump and figure out which piece is vibrating. Unplug the pump and tie one end of the 4-foot-long string securely to this piece.

3. Clamp the aquarium pump to one end of the countertop or table with one of the C-clamps. Use the other C-clap to attach the plastic housing to the countertop or table, about 3 feet (91.4 cm) away from the pump. Drape the string over the plastic housing to hold it off the table. About 3 feet of string should lie parallel to the table with another 6 inches (15.2 cm) hanging over the end of the plastic housing.

4. Poke two holes on opposites sides of the top of the plastic cup with the scissors. Use the 1-foot-long (30.5 cm) string to make a handle for your cup, like a little bucket.

5. Tie the handle you made in step 4 onto the end of the longer string that hangs off the table. Add a couple of spoonfuls of sand to the cup so that the string is pulled taut.

6. Turn on the pump. You should see the length of string above the countertop vibrate.

7. While the pump is on, add one spoonful of sand to the cup at a time, until the vibrating string resembles a jump rope. This is half a wave. Slowly and carefully add sand until it appears that the wave is standing still. A few grains of sand can make a big difference!

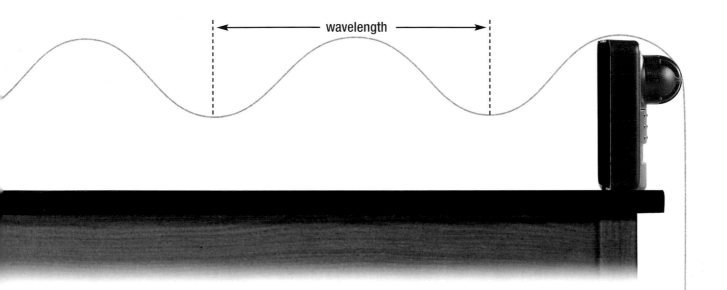

wavelength

8. Remove and weigh the cup of sand. The weight of the sand is equal to the tension on the string. Record the weight of the sand and the number of waves produced.

9. Slowly and carefully remove sand until you see exactly one full wave, and then repeat step 8.

10. Repeat steps 7 through 9, creating one, one and a half, two, two and a half, and three waves. See how many standing waves you can make on your string.

CONCLUSION

How many waves fit on the string? Make a graph of tension versus number of waves. What pattern do you see? How much tension would you need to apply to your string to make 20 standing waves?

TAKE A CLOSER LOOK

The wavelength of the waves on your string depends on the weight of the string, the length of the string, the tension, and the rate at which the string vibrates. Because the pump is plugged into an outlet, it will vibrate 60 times every second. (This is the rate at which electricity pulses from the outlet into the pump.) In this experiment, the rate of vibration, the weight, and the length of the string are kept constant. Tension is the variable that changes the wavelength of the waves on the string.

WHAT ELSE YOU CAN DO

Try using other types of string, such as yarn, twine, cotton, nylon, and fishing line. What effect does length have on vibration? How about the diameter or gauge (thickness) of the string? See what happens if you look at your standing wave with a strobe light.

Wing It

It's impossible to fly without wings, but it's not because of their ability to flap. If you watch a hawk flying, you'll notice that it doesn't really move its wings. Instead, it glides through the air. The shape of a wing is one of the most important factors in how well something can fly.

How does the shape of a wing affect its lift?

EXPERIMENT SUMMARY

You'll design a variety of airplane wings and test their lift with a fan.

WHAT YOU NEED

▶ **Wing tester (see page 81)**
▶ **Ruler**
▶ **Pencil**
▶ **8½ x 11-inch (21.6 cm x 27.9 cm) pieces of paper**
▶ **Tape**
▶ **Small fan**

EXPERIMENTAL PROCEDURE

1. Make the wing tester on page 81.

2. To build your wing, use the ruler and pencil to draw a line on a piece of paper 5 inches (12.7 cm) from the top.

3. Lightly crease the paper on the line you drew. Bring the corners of the paper together and tape the edge. The paper should be curved on the larger side (see figure 1). This is your first wing.

4. Set up the fan. Use the tape to hold the wing tester in front of it.

5. Center the wing over the tester and mark where the two poles should come through. Use the pencil to poke holes straight through both parts of the wing. The holes should be big enough that the wing can slide easily up and down the poles.

Figure 1
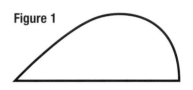

6. Remove the clay from the poles and place your wing on the tester. The curved part of the wing should be on top, facing the fan. Put the clay back on top of the poles.

7. Turn on the fan and observe your wing for 1 minute. Record your observations of its motion. Record the highest point on the poles your wing reaches. Take this measurement from the bottom of the wings.

8. Make at least five more wings to test. Vary the distance from the top of the paper to the crease to create wings with more and less curve on top. Repeat steps 5 through 7 for each wing and record your observations carefully.

CONCLUSION

Which wing flew the highest? Which was most stable? Did any of your wings not even get off the ground? Make a bar graph of wing shape (from most to least curved) versus height reached. Which shape wing would you recommend to a glider designer?

TAKE A CLOSER LOOK

In 1783, Daniel Bernoulli described the effects of fast-moving and slow-moving fluids, such as air. Fast-moving air has less pressure, or less of a push, than slow-moving air. When air strikes your wing, the air must move faster over the top because it has further to go over the curve. This means the slower moving air underneath the wing has a greater push than the faster moving air on top of the wing, causing the airplane to move upwards. This is called lift.

WHAT ELSE YOU CAN DO

Try placing your wings upside down on the wing tester. What other shapes could you test? How do your wings compare to those of birds and airplanes? What happens if you block the top or bottom of the fan so only the top or bottom of your wing is hit with moving air? Try a fan with different speed settings and compare the effects of fast-moving and slow-moving air on your wings.

Making the Wing Tester

WHAT YOU NEED

▸ **5 x 10 inch (12.7 cm x 25.4 cm) piece of cardboard**

▸ **Tape**

▸ **Ruler**

▸ **Pencil**

▸ **2 large bamboo skewers or knitting needles**

▸ **Tape**

▸ **Modeling clay**

WHAT YOU DO

1. Fold the cardboard into a square so that it looks like a box with open ends. Tape it together (see figure 2).

2. With the ruler and pencil, measure and mark off every ½ inch (1.3 cm) on the skewers or knitting needles. You'll use these to measure how high your wing flies.

3. Use the ruler to mark two dots, 3 inches (7.6 cm) apart, in the center of one side of the cardboard square. Poke the skewers or knitting needles through these dots. These will be the poles. Make sure they are straight, and then secure them with tape. They shouldn't move around while you're performing your experiment.

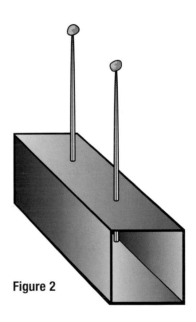

Figure 2

Crash Test Dummies

You know you've always wanted to smash a few dozen eggs. Well, now you have the perfect excuse: it's science! Use eggs and a toy car to test the effectiveness of seat belts.

PROBLEM/PURPOSE

How does wearing a seat belt affect the damage to a passenger in a car crash?

EXPERIMENT SUMMARY

You'll crash a toy car with and without a seat belt and rate the damage done to the egg passenger.

WHAT YOU NEED

- 6-foot-long (1.8 m) board
- Toy car
- Several books
- Wall
- Masking tape
- 2 yardsticks
- 18 large raw eggs
- Resealable plastic bags (optional)
- Stopwatch
- String

EXPERIMENTAL PROCEDURE

1. Use the board to make a ramp for your car. Prop up one end of the board with several books so that it's about 18 inches (45.7 cm) off the ground. The end of the ramp should be 12 inches (30.5 cm) from the wall that the car will crash into.

2. Tape the yardsticks end to end along the center of the board. This will serve as a guide with the wheels of the car running along either side. (Without the guide, the car might go off the side of the ramp.)

3. If you want to eliminate the messy part of breaking eggs, place a raw egg in a resealable plastic bag before putting it in the toy car. You may need to use some small pieces of tape to keep the egg seated in the car. If you do, try not to restrain the egg any more than necessary.

4. Put the car at the top of the ramp and let it go. Don't push the car! Start the stopwatch and time how long it takes for the car to go down the ramp. Stop timing when the car reaches the end of the ramp, not when it hits the wall.

Record your observations of the motion of the egg when it crashes into the wall and the time it took for the car to go down the ramp.

5. Carefully examine the egg. Rank its injuries from 1 to 5 using the damage chart on the right. Record the injuries sustained by the egg.

6. If your first trial resulted in no visible damage, increase the height of your ramp until you see some damage.

7. Repeat steps 3 through 5 with eight more eggs.

8. Use tape and string to make a seat belt for your egg to hold the egg securely in its seat. Repeat steps 3 through 5 with nine eggs.

9. Calculate the average injury ranking for the restrained and unre-strained eggs.

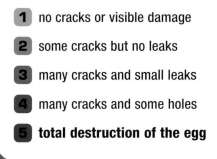

Damage Chart

1 no cracks or visible damage

2 some cracks but no leaks

3 many cracks and small leaks

4 many cracks and some holes

5 **total destruction of the egg**

CONCLUSION

Compare the injury rankings of the restrained and unrestrained eggs. Was there a difference in injuries with and without a seat belt? What did you observe about the motion of your eggs when they crashed into the wall?

TAKE A CLOSER LOOK

Injuries in car crashes are caused by a large *impulse*. Impulse is a combination of force and the time that force is felt. A large force over a short time period, such as in a car crash, will cause a lot of injury to the passengers and damage to the car. By extending the time the wall takes to stop the car or egg, you can decrease the amount of force they experience. Safety features such as seat belts and air bags slow down the passengers a bit more gradually than something hard like the windshield. Therefore, the risk of injury is decreased. Some cars even crumple up in the front and back so the car takes more of the force and the passengers take less.

WHAT ELSE YOU CAN DO

How does speed affect the injuries sustained by the eggs? Adjust the height of the ramp to change the speed. Use a stopwatch to time how long the car takes to roll down the ramp. To calculate the average speed, divide the distance traveled by the time it took the car to go down the ramp. What materials could you place on the wall to decrease the impact to the egg when it crashes? Does the weight or size of the car affect the crash injuries? What if you crash into another moving car instead of stationary wall? What if you crash into a stationary car? What happens to the eggs in the stationary cars?

My whole life flashed before me!

Quick, somebody call 911!!

I can't look. Didn't he know chickens aren't supposed to cross the road?

I saw the whole thing! Man, did he *smack* that wall!

Bending Light

Liquid can do funny things to light. If you stick a straw into a glass of water and then look through the glass, the part of the straw submerged in the water doesn't line up with the part of the straw sticking out of the water.

PROBLEM/PURPOSE

How does the density of different liquids affect how they bend light?

EXPERIMENT SUMMARY

You'll place a penny in different liquids and observe how the liquids bend the light.

WHAT YOU NEED

▶ Bowl with sides 1 to 2 inches (2.5 to 5.1 cm) high and about 6 inches (15.2 cm) wide*

▶ Masking tape

▶ Tape measure

▶ Penny

▶ Marker

▶ Water

▶ Measuring cup

▶ Notebook and pencil

▶ Rubbing alcohol

▶ Cooking oil

Make sure the bowl is not made of clear glass. You want to see the penny by looking down into the bowl.

EXPERIMENTAL PROCEDURE

1. Find the center of the bowl. Stick a piece of tape on the bottom of the outside of the bowl to mark the spot.

2. Use a tape measure to find a spot on the floor with 3 to 4 yards (2.7 to 3.7 m) of walking space behind it. (A hallway would work well.) Place a piece of masking tape on the spot.

3. Place the bottom edge of the bowl on the edge of the piece of masking tape.

4. Put the penny on the mark you made in the center of the bowl.

5. Back away from the bowl until you just lose sight of the penny.

6. Mark this spot on the floor with a piece of tape. Use the marker to label the tape "dry."

7. Fill the bowl one-half to three-quarters full with water. Place the bowl in the exact spot you determined in step 3. Back away from the bowl again until you just lose sight of the penny. Mark this spot with a piece of tape and label it "water."

8. Pour the water from the bowl into the measuring cup and record in your notebook how much water was in the bowl. Dry the bowl, put the penny in it, and put it back where it was in step 3.

9. Repeat step 7 with rubbing alcohol and then with cooking oil, using the same amount of each as the water you measured in step 8. Be sure to clean the bowl before testing the next substance.

10. Measure and record the distance at which the penny disappeared for each liquid.

CONCLUSION

What happens when you add water to the empty bowl? Rank the liquids in order of the amount of *refraction,* or bending, they caused from least to most. The greater the distance at which the penny disappeared, the more the light was bent.

Test the density of the liquids by pouring all three of them into a single clear glass. The more dense liquid will sink to the bottom and the least dense will float to the top. Rank the liquids from most to least dense. Does the amount of refraction relate to the density?

TAKE A CLOSER LOOK

Light *refracts*, or bends, when it travels from one transparent substance to another. The light changes speed when it changes substance, which causes the light to refract. When light moves from a more dense substance to a less dense substance, it speeds up and is bent outward. When it travels from a less dense to a more dense substance, it slows down and bends inward.

However, density is not the only characteristic of matter that creates refraction. You may have noticed that although oil is less dense than water, it causes greater refraction. Color (the wavelength of the light wave) and the interaction of the light's energy with the liquid's molecules also affect the amount of refraction.

WHAT ELSE YOU CAN DO

What other clear liquids could you test? Does the color of the object or of the liquid make a difference in how much the light is bent? Try using red and blue poker chips instead of a penny, or color the water with food coloring.

Balancing Tricks

Girls can do everything boys can do, but can boys do everything girls can do?

PROBLEM/PURPOSE

How does your center of gravity affect your performance on simple balancing tests?

EXPERIMENT SUMMARY

You'll measure the center of gravity of several volunteers and then rate their performance on two balancing tests.

WHAT YOU NEED

- ▶ 2 bathroom scales
- ▶ 2 chairs
- ▶ 6-foot-long (1.8 m) board, at least 6 inches (15.2 cm) wide
- ▶ Measuring tape
- ▶ Masking tape
- ▶ Notebook
- ▶ Marker
- ▶ Equal number of male and female volunteers

EXPERIMENTAL PROCEDURE

1. Place one bathroom scale on each chair and move the chairs about 5 feet (1.5 m) apart. Place the chairs so their backs are away from each other.

2. Place the board so that each end rests on the scales and you can still read the values on the scales. Carefully shift the board back and forth on the scales so that the reading on each scale is the same.

3. Measure the distance between the edges of the scales where the board is no longer supported. Carefully mark the center of this distance on the board with the masking tape. (It will be easier if you mark the edge of the board.)

4. Carefully measure and record in your notebook the height, age, and gender of your first volunteer.

5. Have the volunteer lie on his back on the plank and carefully adjust his position until the reading on both scales is equal. Make sure that no part of the volunteer's body is resting on anything besides the board.

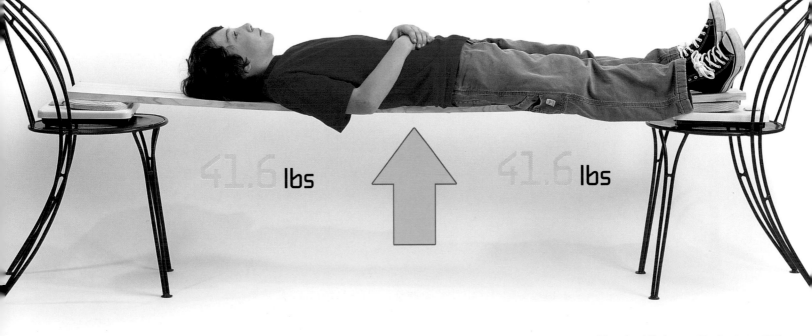

41.6 lbs   41.6 lbs

6. Notice where the halfway mark on the board falls on your volunteer's body. This point is his center of gravity. Stick a piece of masking tape to your volunteer at his center of gravity.

7. Measure and record the distance from the center of gravity of your volunteer to the bottom of his feet.

8. Have your volunteer perform the two balancing tests below. Record what happens.

9. Repeat steps 4 through 8 for each volunteer.

CONCLUSION

Find the midway point for each of your volunteers by dividing his or her height by 2. Compare the center of gravity of each volunteer to his or her midway point. Group the volunteers according to where their center of gravity falls: above their midway point, exactly at their midway point, or below their midway point. How did the volunteers in each group perform on the balancing tests? Is there a relationship between center of gravity and balancing abilities?

The Balancing Tests

Chair Lift

WHAT YOU NEED

▶ **Wall**
▶ **Chair**

WHAT YOU DO

1. With your shoes on, stand exactly two shoe lengths from the wall.

2. Place a chair between you and the wall so that the back of the chair is against the wall.

3. Bend at the waist so that your body makes a right angle, with your head resting against the wall.

4. Grasp the seat of the chair and lift it.

5. Keep both feet flat on the ground and stand upright.

Nose Dive

WHAT YOU NEED

▶ **Empty soda can**

WHAT YOU DO

1. Kneel on the floor and place both your elbows in front of your knees so that your hands point straight out in front of your body.

2. Have a friend place an empty soda can right at your fingertips.

3. Place both of your hands behind your back.

4. Without using your hands, lean forward and nudge the soda can with your nose.

Your *center of gravity* is the center of your weight distribution. In general, small children have a higher center of gravity because of their proportionally larger heads and shorter legs. Men tend to have a higher center of gravity because they have larger shoulders, and women tend to have a lower center of gravity because they have larger hips. In any case, as long as your center of gravity is over your base (for example, your feet when you are standing), you won't fall over.

Volunteers with a higher center of gravity tend to perform worse on the balancing tests. In the Chair Lift exercise, those with a high center of gravity will use their head to balance once their center of gravity moves out from over their feet. When they pick up the chair, they're too top-heavy to stand up. The same idea holds for the Nose Dive exercise. Those with a higher center of gravity quickly fall once they lean far enough forward so that their center of gravity is no longer over their knees.

WHAT ELSE YOU CAN DO

Compare kids and adults. Does center of gravity change with age? What other balancing tests could you try? How does the center of gravity compare to the location of belly buttons?

Belly Buttons

Belly buttons are one of the weirdest features of the human body. No one really understands why some are innies and some are outies. But have you ever wondered why your belly button is located on your belly instead of say, your knee or your chin?

It's pretty simple really. The reason your belly button is where it is has to do with center of gravity. In the Balancing Tricks experiment, you learned that your center of gravity is the center of your weight distribution. It's also the point that something would rotate around if thrown in the air.

For example, take a regular bathroom plunger. The plunger end is heavier than the handle end, right? If you were to measure the center of gravity of the plunger, you would find that it's closer to the plunger end. If you go outside and throw it in the air, you would notice that it wobbles as it spins around. It wobbles because it's spinning around its center of gravity instead of the center of the handle.

This is exactly how people work! If you were to throw a person (do NOT try this!), they too would rotate around their center of gravity.

But what does this have to do with belly buttons?

Your belly button is where the umbilical cord connected to your body when you were still in the womb. You used the umbilical cord to breathe and eat. While you were hanging out in the womb, you were moving around, exploring, and probably kicking and punching your mom while you were at it. Basically, you were a little person rotating around in there. And of course, you rotated around your center of gravity! This is the only place the umbilical cord could attach so that you didn't get all tangled up and cut off your food supply.

Cartoonists are not bound by the laws of physics. Charlie Brown and Calvin are two examples of cartoon kids with unusually large heads and small bodies. If Charlie and Calvin were real people, where would their belly buttons be? If you were to analyze their center of gravity you would find that their belly buttons would have to be located on their chins!

Chemistry

Chemistry always conjures up images of mad scientists mixing together fizzing, boiling, oozing, and steaming liquids. Of course, it's a lot more than that. Chemistry is the study of different forms of matter. Chemists are curious about the structure, composition, properties, and reactions of gases, solids, liquids, and combinations of the three. And what does that mean in the real world? Did you know that you can use diapers to put out forest fires? Want to know how to keep flowers alive for longer? Does hot or cold water freeze faster? And just what is the best way to get ketchup out of the bottle?

Freeze Out

Icy roads make winter driving dangerous. Many places put salt on the roads in the winter. How does this help prevent accidents?

PROBLEM/PURPOSE

How does salt affect the temperature of melting ice?

EXPERIMENT SUMMARY

You'll add salt to crushed ice and measure the temperature to determine the ideal combination of salt for melting ice.

WHAT YOU NEED

- ▶ **Measuring cup**
- ▶ **Crushed ice**
- ▶ **Large styrofoam cup**
- ▶ **Thermometer**
- ▶ **Salt**

EXPERIMENTAL PROCEDURE

1. Put ½ cup (137.8 ml) of crushed ice into the cup.

2. Stick the thermometer into the ice. Hold the cup and stir the ice with the thermometer until a steady temperature is reached.

3. Record this temperature as the normal melting temperature of ice.

4. Add 2 teaspoons (10 ml) of salt to the ice and stir. Continue stirring until the temperature stops dropping.

5. Record the lowest temperature reached.

6. Empty and rinse out your cup. Repeat steps 4 and 5, mixing 1 (5 ml), 4 (20 ml), and 8 teaspoons (40 ml) of salt with ½ cup (137.8 ml) of ice.

7. Try your own combinations of ice and salt to see how low the temperature will go.

CONCLUSION

Make a graph of salt added versus melting temperature. How did the melting temperature of the ice change as you added more salt? What combination of salt and ice gave the lowest melting temperature? How does this affect your ability to make ice cream?

TAKE A CLOSER LOOK

When you add salt to water, you introduce dissolved particles into the water. The freezing point of water (32°F [0°C]) lowers as more particles are added until the point where the salt stops dissolving. For table salt (sodium chloride, NaCl) in water, this temperature can be as low as -6°F (-21°C).

WHAT ELSE YOU CAN DO

What other salts can you use to lower the melting point of ice? Try calcium chloride or even rock salt. Does it make a difference if the ice is already melting?

Fizzability

What do you do when your soda loses its fizz? Plop in a few ice cubes and the bubbles come back! But do bigger ice cubes mean bigger fizz?

PROBLEM/PURPOSE

What size ice cubes make the biggest fizz?

EXPERIMENT SUMMARY

You'll make ice cubes of different sizes and measure the amount of fizz produced.

WHAT YOU NEED

- Ice cubes
- Freezer
- Water
- 5 plates
- Cold, unopened 2-liter soda
- Tall, clean glass
- Stopwatch

EXPERIMENTAL PROCEDURE

1. Take five ice cubes from the freezer and rinse them quickly with cold water. Stick them together on the plate and place the plate in the freezer. They'll freeze together.

2. Do the same with two, three, and four ice cubes so that you make a total of five different size cubes. (Your final cube size will be a single ice cube.)

3. Open the soda and fill the glass three-quarters full. Be sure to replace the cap tightly on the soda bottle.

4. Wait for the initial fizz on the top of the soda to disappear.

5. Remove the largest ice cube from the freezer. Hold it at the top of the glass and drop it in. Start the stopwatch.

6. Time how long the soda fizzes. Record the fizz time.

7. Rinse and dry the glass.

8. Repeat steps 3 through 7 with the remaining ice cubes.

CONCLUSION

Make a graph of ice cube size versus fizz time. Does the amount of fizz depend on the size of the ice cube? What size ice cube gives the best fizz?

TAKE A CLOSER LOOK

Soda gets it fizz when it's carbonated. *Carbonation* is the process in which a gas, such as carbon dioxide, is added to a drink. The fizz in soda is caused when the carbon dioxide gas is released. When you add an ice cube (or any other object) to the soda, it pushes the soda out of the way to make more room in the glass. The level of soda rises in the glass and the gas (which is the carbonation in the soda) gets pushed. This push, or *pressure*, forces the carbon dioxide to bubble out of the soda. The more you push on the soda, such as with a bigger ice cube, the more carbon dioxide is released and the more fizz you get.

Eureka!

If you've ever swum in the ocean or any other salty water, you know that it's much easier to float in salt water. This is because salt water is denser than fresh water. But just how much salt is necessary to make you float?

PROBLEM/PURPOSE

How does the amount of salt in a glass of water affect the ability of different objects to float?

EXPERIMENT SUMMARY

You'll slowly add salt to a glass of water to determine how much is necessary to make various objects float.

WHAT YOU NEED

- ▶ Scale
- ▶ Raw egg
- ▶ Water
- ▶ Large graduated cylinder
- ▶ Large clear bowl
- ▶ Measuring cup
- ▶ ¼ teaspoon
- ▶ Iodized salt
- ▶ Spoon
- ▶ Hardboiled egg
- ▶ Paper clip
- ▶ Small rubber bouncy ball

EXPERIMENTAL PROCEDURE

1. Use the scale to weigh the raw egg. Record its mass in grams. (You'll use the metric scale in this experiment because it makes the calculations easier at the end.)

2. Place 250 milliliters (ml) of water in the graduated cylinder. Place the egg in the water and wait for the egg to sink. Record how much the water rose in the graduated cylinder in milliliters (ml). This tells you the volume of space the egg takes up. (You'll use this measurement to calculate density in step 9.)

3. Fill the bowl with exactly 1000 ml of water. Be sure to use the exact same amount of water for each trial.

4. Place the raw egg in the bowl and wait for it to sink to the bottom.

5. Add ¼ teaspoon (1.6 g) of salt to the bowl and gently mix it into the water using the spoon.

6. Observe the egg. Does it stay on the bottom or does it start to rise in the water? Slowly stir in ¼ teaspoon of salt at a time and observe the egg carefully. Record how much salt was added when the egg first starts to rise off the bottom of the bowl and when it first breaks the surface of the water.

7. Carefully wash and dry the bowl.

8. Repeat steps 1 through 7 for the hardboiled egg, paper clip, and rubber ball.

9. Calculate the density of the various objects by dividing their mass in grams (from step 1) by their volume in milliliters (from step 2). This will give you the density of each object in grams per milliliter.

10. Calculate the density of the water when each object first starts to float and when it breaks the water's surface. The mass of the water is 1000 grams plus 1.6 grams for each ¼ teaspoon of salt. The volume of the water is 1000 milliliters plus 1 milliliter for each ¼ teaspoon of salt. Use the same equation you used in step 9 to calculate the density of the water.

CONCLUSION

Make a bar graph of the density of each object, the density of the water when the object first begins to float, and the density of the water when the object comes to the top of the bowl of water.

Did all of the objects float eventually? Which object required the most salt to float? Which required the least? Did they float to the top immediately or hang out in the middle of the bowl of water for a while? How did the density of the water compare to the density of the object when it began to float? How can you use your data to explain why some objects float and others sink?

TAKE A CLOSER LOOK

Density measures the amount of mass in a given volume, or how much "stuff" is in a certain amount of space. Small, heavy things are more dense than small, light things and much more dense than big, light things.

Objects float when they are less dense than the substance they are immersed in. Helium balloons are less dense than air, so they float. People are denser than air, so they don't float. However, people are about the same density as the salt water in the ocean, so they naturally float somewhere just under the surface of the water. With a little bit of effort you can drift easily in the salt water, although some people are denser than others. Women are usually less dense than men, because they have more fat on their bodies. Muscle is more dense than fat, so your density depends on what type of shape you're in.

Ask your local bowling alley for old 8- and 16-pound (3.6 and 7.3 kg) bowling balls. Fill your bathtub with water and carefully place the balls in the tub. Some bowling balls float! All bowling balls are the same size, but in order to have different weights they have to have different densities. If you had a big enough bathtub, the planet Saturn would float!

Archimedes and the Gold Crown

WHAT ELSE YOU CAN DO

Try adding other substances besides salt to the water, such as sugar, cornstarch, or anything else that dissolves in water. How do these affect the buoyancy of an object? Does the temperature of the liquid affect how much salt is needed to make the different objects float? Try placing the objects in other liquids besides water, such as vinegar, milk, or light corn syrup. What other objects can you float?

Archimedes lived more than 2,000 years ago in Greece. He spent a lot of time inventing crazy machines to help his friend King Hiero of Syracuse (the one in Greece, not in New York) keep out invaders. King Hiero liked to wear crowns and he decided to have a special crown made of pure gold. He placed an order with his local crown maker and sent over the gold.

When the crown was finally delivered, it looked like it was fit for a king, but something didn't seem quite right to King Hiero. He suspected that his crown maker had kept a little gold for himself and mixed in some silver to even it out. King Hiero needed to prove it, so he called on his good friend Archimedes, who was known to have a head for these sorts of things.

At first Archimedes was stumped. He knew how to weigh things like crowns and gold and silver, but the crown maker had been clever enough to make sure that the weight of the crown was exactly the same as the weight of the gold King Hiero had given him. Like many scientists, Archimedes decided to take a warm bath and think over the problem.

His servant and head bath-drawer filled the tub up to the brim. As Archimedes stepped into the tub he noticed that some of the water spilled out of the tub. In fact, the more his body sank into the tub, the more water ran out onto the floor. At first he was annoyed at making such as mess, especially since hot water was hard to come by in Syracuse. But then he had an idea.

Archimedes already knew that silver was less dense than gold. This meant that a crown with gold and silver had to take up more space than a crown of pure gold. If he put the crown in a full bathtub and an equal amount of pure gold in another bathtub, he could compare the amount of water that spilled from each one. "Eureka!" he exclaimed (this means "I have found it" in Greek) and jumped from the tub without so much as a toga on and ran through the streets of Syracuse straight to the king.

Upon reaching the king, he was quickly given a robe, and he demonstrated his findings with the crown. Unfortunately for the crown maker, the king's suspicions were correct and Archimedes had proven that some of the gold was stolen. Archimedes went on to develop *Archimedes' Principle of Buoyancy* and his work "On Floating Bodies." King Hiero went on to briefly lead a prosperous kingdom until Archimedes' war machines failed him and invaders conquered his realm. The crown maker's fate is unknown but I don't think he received many recommendations from King Hiero.

Cold Packs

When you sprain an ankle or get hit in the head, the first the thing the doctor will tell you to do is put some ice on it. Because ice is solid and usually square, it's kind of hard to wrap around your ankle. Instead, you put a cold pack on your ankle. A cold pack uses a chemical reaction to cool down the water inside it and thus better conform to your ankle.

PROBLEM/PURPOSE

How do different chemicals affect the temperature of water?

EXPERIMENT SUMMARY

You'll add various chemicals to water and measure the change in temperature.

WHAT YOU NEED

- ► Water
- ► Measuring spoon and cup
- ► Plastic cups
- ► Thermometer
- ► Sodium bicarbonate (baking soda)*
- ► Citric acid (sour salt)*
- ► Potassium chloride (Morton Lite, used as a substitute for table salt)*
- ► Sodium carbonate (washing soda)*
- ► Calcium chloride (deicer)*

You can find these at the grocery or hardware store.

Next year I *better* get a top locker!

EXPERIMENTAL PROCEDURE

1. Add ½ cup (136.8 ml ml) of water to a plastic cup.

2. Use the thermometer to measure the temperature of the water. Record the value. Leave the thermometer in the cup.

3. Quickly add 1 teaspoon (5 ml) of sodium bicarbonate to the cup of water and stir it gently with the thermometer.

4. When the sodium bicarbonate is completely dissolved, read and record the temperature.

5. Calculate the change in temperature by subtracting the starting temperature from the final temperature of the water. Record the change in temperature.

6. Wash and dry the cup and thermometer. Repeat steps 1 through 5, using 2 teaspoons (10 ml), 4 teaspoons (20 ml), and then 2 tablespoons (30 ml) of sodium bicarbonate.

7. Repeat steps 1 through 6 using the citric acid, potassium chloride, sodium carbonate, and calcium chloride.

CONCLUSION

Make a graph of the amount of powder versus temperature change for each of the chemicals. Which chemical caused the biggest temperature change? How many teaspoons (milliliters) did you add to get the largest temperature change? Which solution would make the best cold pack?

TAKE A CLOSER LOOK

A lot of cold packs mix water with a chemical that causes the temperature of the water to drop. This is called an *endothermic reaction.*

Salts and sodas are made of molecules. A *molecule* is a group of atoms attached together by a chemical force. If you look carefully at the salts, you can see small crystals, which are a bunch of molecules clumped together. When salts and sodas are added to water, they *ionize*. This means the molecule splits into two or more charged atoms, or groups of atoms called *ions*. Each ion has a positive or negative charge. For example, calcium chloride splits up into a positively charged calcium ion and a negatively charged chloride ion. If the process of breaking apart the molecules uses up energy, the solution gets colder. In this case, the heat of the solution is called an endothermic reaction. If energy is released when the molecules break apart, the solution becomes warmer. In this case, the heat of the

solution is called an *exothermic reaction.* In general, the more chemical you add to the water, the more ions are formed. This means more energy is used or released, so there is a greater temperature change.

WHAT ELSE YOU CAN DO

Try different ratios of chemicals and water. Is there a limit to how cold the solutions can get? What happens when you add both calcium chloride and sodium bicarbonate to the water? Will other chemicals, such as sodium chloride (table salt) or even sugar, cause a change in temperature? Which chemicals could be used to make the water heat up?

Sorry, it was an accident!

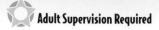

Fighting Fire with Diapers?

Disposable diapers have more uses than they were intended for. During a house fire, one firefighter noticed that the only thing that wasn't burning was the diaper pail. How do diapers stack up against other flame-retardant materials?

PROBLEM/PURPOSE

Which materials are the most flame retardant?

EXPERIMENT SUMMARY

You'll test water, sodium polyacrylate, and a flame-retardant fabric to see which takes longer to start burning.

WHAT YOU NEED

- Scissors
- Disposable diaper
- Resealable plastic bag
- Cups
- Measuring spoons and cups
- Water
- Spoon
- Lighter or matches
- Candle
- 24 wood splints
- Stopwatch
- Flame-retardant fabric*

Children's Halloween costumes are often made of flame-retardant fabric.

SAFETY: Wash your hands carefully after handling sodium polyacrylate. Be careful not to inhale the powder. Always have an adult present when dealing with an open flame. Don't wear loose clothing. If you have long hair, tie it back.

EXPERIMENTAL PROCEDURE

1. With scissors, cut open a new disposable diaper and shake the stuffing into a resealable plastic bag.

2. Place 1 teaspoon (5 ml) of diaper stuffing (sodium polyacrylate) into a cup. Add ½ cup (137.8 ml) of water to the powder and stir the mixture with the spoon until it forms a gel. Record your observations.

3. Light the candle. Keep a glass of water nearby to extinguish the splints.

4. Place the end of a dry wood splint into the flame. Use the stopwatch to time how long it takes to catch fire. Extinguish the splint in the glass of water and record the time.

5. Repeat step 4 five more times, using a new splint each time. Calculate the average ignition time.

6. Soak six splints in a glass of water for 3 minutes. Repeat steps 4 and 5 using the water-soaked splints.

7. Soak six splints in the polyacrylate solution for 3 minutes. Repeat steps 4 and 5 using these splints.

8. Tie a small piece of flame-retardant fabric to six splints. Repeat steps 4 and 5 using these splints.

CONCLUSION

Make a graph of the material versus the average ignition time. Which material burned fastest? Slowest? Which material is the most flame retardant? What are potential hazards and benefits of using sodium polyacrylate to prevent fires?

TAKE A CLOSER LOOK

Sodium polyacrylate is used in diapers because it absorbs many times its weight in water. The absorbed water prevents the splint from burning. The splint soaked in just water will burn faster because the water quickly evaporates in the flame. The sodium polyacrylate holds onto the water longer, keeping the splint coated in water. Scientists are working on a system to spray a sodium polyacrylate/water solution on homes to protect them from nearby forest fires.

WHAT ELSE YOU CAN DO

What other materials could you test? Will the water and sodium polyacrylate work as well if they are soaked for more or less time? What effect does adding more water to the sodium polyacrylate solution have?

QUICK, make your choice, fella! The fire's a blazin'!

Flower Power

Cut flowers are only pretty when they're fresh. Once they start to wilt and die, they turn brown and start smelling bad. How can you keep cut flowers looking lovely longer?

PROBLEM/PURPOSE

How do different additives affect the freshness of flowers?

EXPERIMENT SUMMARY

You'll add a variety of chemical additives to the water of fresh-cut flowers to see how long it takes the flowers to wilt.

WHAT YOU NEED

► 6 clean 2-liter bottles
► Water
► Commercial additive*
► Measuring cups and spoons
► Bleach
► Sugar
► Vinegar
► Lemon-lime soda (regular, not diet)
► Mouthwash
► Penny
► Aspirin tablet
► Scissors
► 2 dozen identical cut flowers
► Camera (optional)

*This usually comes with cut flowers.
Ask a florist if you can have a few packets.*

EXPERIMENTAL PROCEDURE

1. Fill one bottle with water. This will be your control. Empty and refill the bottle with clean water every day.

2. Fill the rest of the bottles with the recipes from the chart (see page 101).

3. Use the scissors to cut 1 inch (2.5 cm) off the end of each of the flowers. Put four flowers into each bottle.

4. Place the flowers in a cool room out of direct sunlight.

5. Monitor the flowers each day and record your observations. Add water to the bottles if the levels become low. You may want to take photographs. Record the time and date that each of the four flowers in the bottles show signs of wilting. Record the time and date when all the flowers in each bottle are dead.

CONCLUSION

Make a graph of how long it took the flowers to wilt for each type of solution. If the four flowers in a particular bottle wilted at different times, use the average time. Which recipe was best at keeping the flowers fresh? Which was worst? What other observations did you make?

TAKE A CLOSER LOOK

Most floral preservatives contain three important things:

1. An energy source, such as sugar.

2. An acid to prevent the flower stems from becoming blocked. These stem blockages keep the flowers from taking in water, causing the flowers to wilt.

3. A bactericide to kill bacteria and fungi. Bacteria can come from dirt in the vase and may exist naturally on the stem and can cause the stems to become blocked.

Which of the ingredients in the recipes were the energy source, the acid, and the bactericide?

WHAT ELSE YOU CAN DO

How might you modify or improve the recipes to get better results? Call some local florists or talk to friends and family and ask whether they have any other recipes for keeping flowers fresh. Try them out and see what happens.

Solution Chart

Bottle 1: Add the commercial preservative pack and fill the bottle with water. Follow the instructions on the packet.

Bottle 2: Add ½ teaspoon (2.5 ml) of bleach, 3 tablespoons (45 ml) of sugar, and 4 teaspoons (20 ml) of vinegar to the bottle. Fill the rest of the bottle with water.

Bottle 3: Add half a liter of lemon-lime soda and ½ teaspoon (2.5 ml) of bleach to the bottle. Fill the rest of the bottle with water. Every 4 days add another ¼ teaspoon (1.3 ml) of bleach.

Bottle 4: Fill the bottle with water and add ¼ cup (.1 l) of mouthwash.

Bottle 5: Fill the bottle with water. Add a penny and one aspirin tablet.

Light Sticks

Have you seen a firefly glow at dusk? They use a chemical reaction to produce light. In a light stick this reaction is called *chemiluminescence*. Is chemiluminescence affected by temperature?

PROBLEM/PURPOSE

How is the brightness of light sticks affected by temperature?

EXPERIMENT SUMMARY

You'll activate light sticks at different temperatures and rank their brightness.

WHAT YOU NEED

▶ **5 light sticks, all the same color**
▶ **Permanent marker**
▶ **4 tall styrofoam cups**
▶ **Hot (but not boiling) water**
▶ **Warm water**
▶ **Cold water**　　▶ **Stopwatch**
▶ **Ice water**　　▶ **2 helpers**
▶ **4 thermometers**　▶ **Refrigerator**

> **SAFETY:** *Don't break or cut open the light sticks. The chemicals may be hazardous. Never put a light stick in the microwave or oven.*

EXPERIMENTAL PROCEDURE

1. Use the permanent marker to label the cups "hot," "warm," "cold," and "ice." Pour the hot, warm, cold, and ice water into the corresponding cups. Make sure the water is deep enough to cover at least two-thirds of the light stick.

2. Place a thermometer in each cup. Start the stopwatch. After 1 minute record the temperatures. The temperature of each cup should be at least 15 degrees F apart. Add ice or hot water to the cups if they aren't.

3. Following the directions on the light stick package, have your helpers activate each stick. Start the stopwatch and record the time you activated them.

4. Place one light stick in each cup of water and stir it. It helps to do all the light sticks at the same time so you can compare their brightness, so have your helpers each stir two light sticks.

5. After stirring the light sticks for 1 minute, compare their brightness. Turn out the lights to examine the light sticks. Record your observations and the temperature of the water.

6. Put the light sticks back in the cups and stir for 5 more minutes. Compare the brightness of the light sticks. Record your observations and the temperature of the water as you did in step 5.

7. Leave the light sticks in their cups for 1 hour. Compare the brightness of the light sticks. Record your observations and the temperature of the water.

8. Place the cup labeled "ice" in the refrigerator. Put the cup labeled "hot" on top of the refrigerator (where it is warmer). For the other two sticks, you may want to find other spots with varying temperatures, such as by a heater or in front of a fan.

9. Check on the light sticks every 4 to 6 hours. Record the temperature of the water and your observations about the brightness of the light sticks. Be sure to record the time when the light sticks stop glowing.

CONCLUSION

Were there any differences in brightness between the sticks at the beginning of your experiment? After 1 minute at different temperatures? After 5 minutes? After 1 hour? At which temperature did the light stick last the longest? How does temperature affect the brightness of light sticks? How does it affect the life of light sticks?

TAKE A CLOSER LOOK

Light sticks are made of a plastic tube that contains hydrogen peroxide. Inside the tube is a glass vial that contains another chemical, phenyl oxalate ester, and a fluorescent dye, which determines the color. When you break the glass vial inside the tube, the two chemicals mix and a chemical reaction takes place, releasing light.

You may have noticed that the stick does not get hot when it's glowing. This is because the chemical reaction is very efficient and almost all of the energy is released as light. In lightbulbs and most other things that light up, the light is not created by a chemical reaction and only a small bit of the energy is given off as light. The rest is turned into heat.

Using heat to add extra energy to the light stick will speed up the reaction, causing the stick to glow brighter, but for a shorter amount of time. If you cool the light stick, the reaction will slow down, and the light will dim. If you want to preserve your light stick for the next day, put it in the freezer. It won't stop the chemical reaction, but it will slow down the process considerably.

WHAT ELSE YOU CAN DO

How could you quantify or measure the brightness of the light sticks? Does the color of the light stick affect its brightness, reaction to temperature, or length of time it glows?

Fireflies

What Are Fireflies?

Fireflies aren't really flies, they're beetles! Flies have one pair of wings (like houseflies) but all other flying insects have four or two pairs of wings like fireflies. In fact fireflies aren't the only misnamed insects—dragonflies and scorpionflies aren't really flies either.

Fireflies go by other names as well, such as lightning bug or glowworm. Scientists usually give insects and other critters Greek or Latin names and over the years they have come up with some crazy names for fireflies.

Lamprocera - brilliant and wax-colored
Pyrogaster - fire stomach
Pyropyga - fire rump/butt
Microphotus - small light
Lampyris - Glowworm

Why Do They Glow?

Fireflies use a chemical reaction in their *photic organ* (light organ) in their tail. When chemical reactions are used to produce light in organisms it is called *bioluminescence*. In firefly larvae, the bioluminescence is to warn other bugs and animals that want to eat them that the larvae taste bad. When fireflies become adults they use complex flashing patterns to attract mates.

Scientists are interested in how fireflies produce light because it's very efficient. Almost 100 percent of the energy is converted to light, unlike a light bulb where only 10 percent of the energy becomes light and the rest is turned into heat. Imagine what would happen if fireflies got as hot as a light bulb!

How Can I Find Fireflies?

First you need to be in the right part of the country in the summer. If you live west of Kansas you'll have a harder time finding fireflies. The best place to look is on the edges of streams and ponds at night. Fireflies prefer areas where there is plenty of water, so if you happen to be in the tropical forests of Central or South America you should have no trouble.

If you're trying to attract fireflies to your yard, here are some helpful tips:

1. Don't use chemical fertilizers or insecticides on your lawn.

2. Get rid of any lights outside since they will make it harder for fireflies to see each other at night. This is why you don't see many fireflies flashing on clear nights when the moon is full.

3. Make sure you have tall grass or low trees to provide fireflies with a cool place to rest during the day.

Ice Cubes

In the summer, an ice cold drink really hits the spot. But when you run out of ice cubes, it can seem like forever before the water freezes to make more ice. How can you make ice more quickly?

PROBLEM/PURPOSE

How does the temperature of water affect the time it takes to make ice cubes?

EXPERIMENT SUMMARY

You'll make ice cubes from water at different temperatures and time how long it takes them to freeze.

WHAT YOU NEED

▶ **5 thermometers**
▶ **Freezer**
▶ **Stopwatch**
▶ **4 ice cube trays**
▶ **Permanent marker**
▶ **Masking tape**
▶ **Stove**
▶ **4-cup (1 l) glass measuring cup**
▶ **Water**
▶ **Teakettle**

EXPERIMENTAL PROCEDURE

1. Place one of the thermometers in the freezer. Start the stopwatch. Record the temperature after 10 minutes.

2. Label each of the ice cube trays from 1 to 4 with the permanent marker and masking tape.

3. On the stove, boil 4 cups (1 l) of water in the teakettle.

4. In the measuring cup, pour 1 cup (275.5 ml) of boiling water and 2 cups (.5 l) of cold water from the faucet. Place a thermometer in the cup and record the temperature after 1 minute.

5. Pour the water into the first ice cube tray. Stick a thermometer in one of the cube wells and then put the tray in the freezer. Record the time you place the tray in the freezer.

6. Repeat steps 4 and 5, filling three more trays with the following: 2 cups (.5 l) of boiling water and 1 cup (275.5 ml) of cold water mixed together; cold water only; and boiling water only. Reboil the water every time to make sure the water is at the same temperature for each trial. Be sure to record which tray has which temperature water and what time you put the tray in the freezer.

TAKE A CLOSER LOOK

Water will take longer to freeze if it has other substances, such as salt, sugar, or even air, dissolved in it. Hot or boiling water has much less air dissolved in it than cold water. The bubbling of the water as it boils brings the air to the surface and removes it from the water. For this reason, hot water often freezes faster than cold water and salt water will take even longer to freeze.

WHAT ELSE YOU CAN DO

What effect does adding salt or sugar have on the freezing time of water? Try using juice and make popsicles. Does the color of the water make a difference? How does the temperature of the freezer affect freezing time? How about the temperature of the ice cube trays? What other factors do you think might affect freezing time?

7. Check on the trays every 5 minutes. Read the temperature of the water on the thermometer that you put in the ice cube tray in step 5. Record the time and temperature when ice first starts to form on top of the cubes and then again when the cubes are completely frozen.

8. Use the times you recorded to calculate the time it took each tray to begin to freeze and then to freeze completely.

CONCLUSION

Make a graph of water temperature versus freezing time. Which water temperature took the longest to freeze? Which froze the quickest? Which took the most time and the least time to start to freeze? How do these compare? What other observations did you make about how the water froze?

The Ketchup Conundrum

There's nothing more frustrating than trying to get the ketchup to come out of the bottle. And why does it always make a big splat all over your fries when it finally does come out? Are you supposed to hit the bottom, tap the side, or shake it? Is there a better way to get ketchup out of the bottle?

PROBLEM/PURPOSE

How does the thickness of ketchup change when it has been sitting still and when it has been stirred?

EXPERIMENT SUMMARY

You'll time how long it takes various weights to fall through still and stirred ketchup.

WHAT YOU NEED

▶ Bottle of ketchup

▶ Large, clear glass

▶ Ring stand* or 2 clear glasses

▶ Mirror

▶ 10-gram fishing weights or steel balls

▶ Stopwatch

▶ Spoon

*You can order a ring stand from a science supply company or borrow one from your science teacher.

EXPERIMENTAL PROCEDURE

1. Pour the ketchup into the large, clear glass so it's almost full.

2. Put the glass on the ring stand with the mirror underneath. The mirror is there so you can see when the weights reach the bottom without standing on your head. You can put a glass upside down on the mirror and stack a glass with ketchup in it on top instead of using a ring stand (see figure on page 107). Let the ketchup sit for 1 hour.

3. Drop a weight into the ketchup from just above the surface. (You don't want the weight to fall through the air at all.) Make sure the weight is not going to hit the sides of the glass. Use the stopwatch to time how long it takes to reach the bottom. Record the time.

4. Repeat step 3 with four more weights. Be careful not to drop a weight in the same spot where you previously put one. You want each weight to fall through undisturbed ketchup. Make sure you drop the weights from the same height each time. (Don't drop them too close to the edge of the glass, though.)

5. Retrieve the weights with the spoon.

6. Stir the ketchup vigorously for 1 minute, then repeat steps 3 and 4.

CONCLUSION

Average the time it took for each of the five weights to fall through the still and stirred ketchup. Compare the average times. Which is more *viscous* (thicker)? Which do you think would pour out of a bottle easier, still or stirred ketchup? What are some good strategies for getting ketchup to flow easily out of the bottle?

TAKE A CLOSER LOOK

Ketchup is *thixotropic*. That means that when it has been sitting for a while it acts more like a solid. Once it has been stirred up it acts more like a liquid. Ketchup that has been standing still is thicker, or more viscous, than ketchup that has been stirred or shaken. Scientists think that some of this thixotropy comes from the mashed-up tomatoes. The tiny, solid pieces of the tomato form suspended microfibers, like little threads floating in the ketchup. When the ketchup stands still, the fibers touch each other and stick together. This forms a gel in the liquid that gets stronger with time. So if you want to get your ketchup out of the bottle faster, shake it up or stir it with a knife to separate the microfibers.

WHAT ELSE YOU CAN DO

Try stirring the ketchup or letting it sit for different amounts of time. Vary the size of the weights you use. Are there any weights that fall at the same rate regardless of how much the ketchup has been stirred? Are there any weights that never make it to the bottom? Test other strategies for getting ketchup to flow easily out of the bottle.

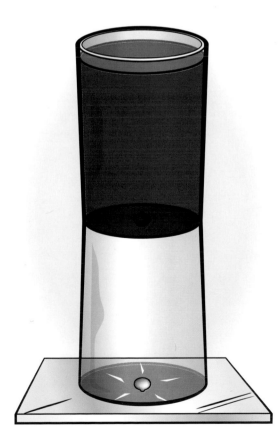

Surface Tension

Have you ever noticed a water strider sliding across a still pond? The strong surface tension of water supports this aquatic insect. Surface tension is a force that holds the surface of a liquid together.

PROBLEM/PURPOSE

How does adding soap to water affect the water's surface tension?

EXPERIMENT SUMMARY

You'll use a button balance to measure and compare the surface tensions of water with different amounts of soap.

WHAT YOU NEED

▶ **Button balance (see page 109)**
▶ **Scissors**
▶ **Paper**
▶ **New disposable plastic cup**
▶ **Water**
▶ **Dishwashing soap**

EXPERIMENTAL PROCEDURE

1. Make the button balance on page 109.

2. Cut at least 20 ½-inch-square (1.3 cm) pieces of paper. These will be the weights you use to measure the surface tension.

3. Fill a cup with clean water.

4. Raise your cup carefully so that the button settles gently on the water's surface. (You'll know it's in place if you lower the cup slightly and the lever tips downward.)

5. Add the small squares of paper, one at a time, until the button comes off the surface of the water. Try to put the button back on the liquid surface. Make sure that it's the weight that has pulled the button off the water rather than the force of dropping the paper into the basket.

6. Count the number of papers needed to pull the button off the water. Record the number.

7. Dry off the button and repeat steps 5 and 6 at least four more times with clean water. Be sure to check that the craft stick is balanced between each trial. Calculate the average number of pieces of paper it took to break the surface tension of the water.

8. Add one drop of dishwashing soap to the cup of water. Repeat steps 4 through 7.

9. Repeat step 8, adding another drop of dishwashing soap to the cup each time. Continue until you've tested at least six drops of soap.

CONCLUSION

Average the number of pieces of paper needed to pull the button off the surface of the water for each trial. This value represents the surface tension, which is the force needed to break the surface of the water. How precise is the button balance? Do you get similar values for surface tension for all the trials for each liquid, or do they vary? (See the error sidebar on page 16.) Make a graph of number of papers versus drops of soap. How did the surface tension change as you added soap to the water? Can you predict how many pieces of paper would be needed to lift the button from water with 10 drops of soap?

TAKE A CLOSER LOOK

Water is a *polar molecule*. That means it has a negatively charged end and a positively charged end. Because opposites attract, water molecules arrange themselves positive end to negative end. This forms a "net" of molecules over the surface of the water that's difficult for small, lightweight objects, such as buttons and water striders, to break. Soap molecules are made of long chains that are *hydrophobic* (repelled by water) at one end and *hydrophilic* (attracted to water) at the other end. When you put a drop of soap into a glass of water, the soap molecules stand up with their hydrophobic ends pointing up to the surface. This breaks up the net of water molecules, making it easier to break the surface tension of the water.

Try testing other liquids, such as rubbing alcohol, vinegar, and salt water. How does hot water compare to cold water? Does the size of the button or the material it's made of matter?

Making a Button Balance

WHAT YOU NEED

- ▶ **Hammer**
- ▶ **Nail**
- ▶ **Craft stick**
- ▶ **Ruler**
- ▶ **Scissors**
- ▶ **Fishing line or nylon string**
- ▶ **Flat button**
- ▶ **Index card**
- ▶ **Chair**
- ▶ **Clay**

WHAT YOU DO

1. Use the hammer and nail to make three holes in the craft stick. Make one hole in the middle and the others about ½ inch (1.3 cm) from each end.

2. Use the ruler and scissors to measure and cut a 14-inch (35.6 cm) piece of string. Loop the string through two of the holes in the button so that it will land parallel to the floor. Tie the other end of the string to the hole on one end of the craft stick so the button hangs about 6 inches (15.2 cm) below the stick.

3. Cut a 3-inch (7.6 cm) square from the index card. Use the nail to poke a hole in each corner of the card.

4. Cut another piece of string and run it through the holes in the index card to make a small basket. Tie the basket to the other end of the craft stick. This basket will act as a counterweight to the button so that the craft stick balances.

5. Tie another piece of string through the middle hole in the craft stick and suspend your balance from a cupboard or chair so that it hangs freely.

6. Use a small piece of clay to balance the craft stick so it hangs horizontally.

The O-Zone

During the summer, you hear a lot about ozone alerts. These are times when dangerous stuff is hanging out in the air, keeping you and your friends from going outside to play. Are there places where bad ozone tends to hang out?

PROBLEM/PURPOSE

What factors affect the amount of ozone in the air?

EXPERIMENT SUMMARY

You'll measure the amount of ozone in the air with ozone test papers placed in different locations.

WHAT YOU NEED

▶ **Ozone test papers (see page 112)**
▶ **Map of the area where you will test the ozone**
▶ **Spray bottle**
▶ **Distilled water**
▶ **Tape**
▶ **Resealable plastic bag**
▶ **Marker**
▶ **Notebook and pencil**

EXPERIMENTAL PROCEDURE

1. Make the ozone test papers on page 112.

2. Examine the map of the area where you'll test the ozone. This could be around your house, in your neighborhood, or around your school. Mark the places where you'll collect data. Don't forget to test indoor and outdoor locations.

3. Choose spots in the test locations where your test strip won't be disturbed for at least 8 hours. It's very important that the paper be out of direct sunlight and can hang freely. You'll get better results on days when it isn't very humid.

4. Spray one of the ozone test strips with distilled water and hang it at a data collection site with a small piece of tape.

5. Repeat step 4 for each of your test sites.

6. Let the ozone test strips hang for about 8 hours.

7. Collect the ozone test strips and seal each one in a plastic bag. Use a marker to label each plastic bag with the location.

8. To see the results, open the bag, spray the paper with distilled water, and observe the color. Compare the color of your strip to the illustration on page 111. Record the data.

CONCLUSION

Rank your locations from lowest to highest ozone levels. Which areas had the highest ozone levels? Why do you think that might be? What about the lower levels? Mark the ozone levels on your map. Can you detect a pattern? Is this a good way to measure ozone in the atmosphere?

TAKE A CLOSER LOOK

Some ozone occurs naturally in the air and some ozone is produced when cars and other machines, such as electric mixers and copy machines, *ionize* oxygen in the air. The oxygen molecules we breathe consist of two oxygen atoms bound together. An ozone molecule has three oxygen atoms bound together. When the oxygen in the air is ionized, the two oxygen atoms are split. Then they join other oxygen molecules to form ozone. So, for every one molecule of oxygen that gets ionized, two molecules of ozone are formed.

Ozone occurs in two layers of the atmosphere. The layer closest to the Earth's surface is the *troposphere*, which reaches 6 miles (9.7 km) up from the ground. Here, ground-level ozone, or "bad," ozone, is an air pollutant found in smog. It's harmful to breathe and damages crops, trees, and plants. The *stratosphere*, or "good" ozone layer, is the next part of the atmosphere. It reaches 25 miles (40.2 km) above the troposphere. The ozone in the strato-

sphere protects life on Earth from the sun's harmful ultraviolet (UV) rays, which cause skin cancer.

The ozone test papers use a chemical reaction to detect the ozone in the air. Ozone reacts with the potassium iodide in the test papers and the water you add to produce oxygen, iodine, and potassium hydroxide. The iodine then reacts with the cornstarch in the paper to create the purple color.

WHAT ELSE YOU CAN DO

What other factors do you think affect ozone levels? How about time of day, temperature, humidity, and time of year? What about other pollutants in the air, such as carbon monoxide, nitrogen dioxide, and sulfur dioxide? Go online and locate ozone data for you area. Compare your results to those reported by local weather services. Based on your experiment and research, see whether you can predict the ozone levels in other locations. Test your predictions.

Ozone test paper

High Ozone

Low Ozone

No Ozone

Making the Ozone Test Papers

WHAT YOU NEED

- **Measuring cup and spoons**
- **Distilled water**
- **Glass bowl or pot (will be used on the stovetop)**
- **Cornstarch**
- **Stovetop**
- **Wooden spoon**
- **Potassium iodide (KI)***
- **Plastic spoon**
- **Scissors**
- **Coffee filters**
- **Glass or ceramic plate**
- **Small paintbrush**
- **Paper**
- **Resealable plastic bag**

You can order this from a chemical supply company or your science teacher may have some.

WHAT YOU DO

1. Put 4 cups (1 l) of distilled water in the glass bowl or pot. (Don't use a metal pot because it will react with the chemicals.)

2. Add 1¼ teaspoon (6.3 ml) of cornstarch.

3. Heat the mixture on the stovetop, stirring it constantly with the wooden spoon, until it thickens and becomes somewhat translucent.

4. Remove the pot from the stove and add ¼ teaspoon (1.3 ml) of potassium iodide (KI). Stir the mixture with the plastic spoon.

5. Let the paste cool in the pot. With scissors, cut the coffee filters open so there's only one layer of paper.

6. Lay a coffee filter on a glass or ceramic plate. Carefully brush the paste onto both sides of the filter with the small paintbrush. Try to apply the paste as uniformly as possible.

7. Make as many papers as you have paste. (It's better to have too many test papers than too few.) Wash your hands well when you're through. Potassium iodide is not toxic but it can cause mild skin irritation.

8. Lay the filter papers on a piece of plain paper in a dark, dry place to dry out.

9. When the papers are dry, use the scissors to cut them into 1-inch (2.5 cm) strips. Wash your hands well.

10. To store the papers, place them in a resealable plastic bag and keep them in a dark place.

Watch out for that bad ozone! But keep the good stuff around!

Make Your Mark

Many markers and pens claim to be indelible or permanent. Just how permanent are permanent markers?

PROBLEM/PURPOSE

How do the marks from different brands of permanent markers react to being washed in soap and water?

EXPERIMENT SUMMARY

You'll mark cloth with several permanent markers and attempt to remove the ink with soap and water.

WHAT YOU NEED

▸ **6 different types of permanent markers**

▸ **Masking tape**

▸ **12 pieces of identical cloth, each 6 inches (15.2 cm) square**

▸ **Washing machine**

▸ **Laundry detergent**

▸ **Camera (optional)**

SAFETY: Permanent markers use a solvent-based ink, and with some brands this solvent is toxic. Read the labels and instructions carefully.

EXPERIMENTAL PROCEDURE

1. Label the markers 1 through 6 with the masking tape.

2. Use each marker to mark on two pieces of cloth. Write the marker's number on the corner of the cloth for identification. Let the ink dry.

3. Separate the cloths into two piles of six cloths. Each pile should have a cloth from each marker.

4. Set one pile aside. This will be the control that you will compare to the washed cloths.

5. Place the other pile of cloths in the washing machine, add the detergent, and run the load through a regular cycle with hot water.

6. Remove the cloths and order them from darkest to lightest. Compare the washed cloths to the originals. Be sure to note the color as well as the lightness of the mark. Record your observations.

7. Repeat steps 5 and 6 at least two more times.

CONCLUSION

Which marker is the most permanent? Did any of the marks change color? Did the marks fade or change color at different rates? Did any of the marks disappear completely? Which marker would you recommend for marking on cloth?

TAKE A CLOSER LOOK

With markers, the name "permanent" means that the ink cannot be washed off with water. You may notice that the ink from a ballpoint pen will run if the paper or cloth you wrote on gets wet. The ink in the pen is water soluble. The inks are mixed together with a small amount of water. When you add more water, the ink gets diluted. The ink in permanent markers is mixed with a liquid other than water. That liquid is called a *solvent*. In many cases, the solvent is a type of alcohol. Usually ink can be washed off with the same or a similar solvent that is used to make the ink.

Misguided Termites

Ants and termites can't see very well, yet they always know exactly where to go. They leave a trail of chemicals for the others to follow. Can you fool termites with ink from pens?

1. On a clean piece of paper, use one of the pens, markers, or pencils to draw a large circle. Record the type of pen you have used.

2. Use the tweezers to carefully place two termites on the paper near the circle.

PROBLEM/PURPOSE

How do different types of ink affect the behavior of termites?

3. Record the behavior of the termites. Do they stay on the paper? Do they follow each other? How do they react to the line you have drawn?

4. Repeat steps 1 through 3 for each of the pens, markers, and pencils. Use a different piece of paper and pair of termites each time.

EXPERIMENT SUMMARY

You'll test several types of inks and observe the reaction of termites.

WHAT YOU NEED

▶ **Paper**
▶ **A variety of pens, markers, and pencils, including Bic and PaperMate pens**
▶ **Tweezers**
▶ **Several termites***

* To find termites, visit a wooded area and look in rotting logs or under wet leaves. Termites look like small white ants. Store the termites in a self-sealing plastic container filled with damp leaves or paper towels. As long you don't capture the queen you don't need to worry about termites infesting your home. (She's much larger and rounder than the rest of the termites.) You can also order termites from science supply companies.

CONCLUSION

Which pens produced lines that the termites followed? What other reactions did you observe? Did the termites appear to be repelled by any of the inks?

TAKE A CLOSER LOOK

Pheromones are chemicals that insects and animals release to communicate. Pheromones signal alarm and attraction, and mark trails for others to follow. Each termite deposits a small amount of pheromone onto the paper or whatever it happens to be walking on. Other termites "smell" the pheromone and react by following the trail, fleeing danger, or finding a mate. Some ink pens contain a compound very similar to the pheromone termites use to mark their trails.

WHAT ELSE YOU CAN DO

Try making a circle with some missing segments. Are the termites able to locate the rest of the path? How far apart can the segments be? What happens when two lines intersect? Do termites follow only fresh ink paths, or does the ink path have the same effect when it is a couple of hours old? Do other insects, such as ants, react to the same types of inks?

"Whiter Teeth in Just One Week!"

Nobody wants nasty brown teeth. How well do whitening toothpastes get rid of stains?

PROBLEM/PURPOSE

How do different whitening toothpastes affect the whiteness of teeth?

EXPERIMENT SUMMARY

You'll stain ceramic tiles with coffee and use whitening toothpastes to clean them.

WHAT YOU NEED

- ▶ 5 ceramic tiles (make sure at least one side is unfinished)
- ▶ Bowl
- ▶ Instant coffee
- ▶ Masking tape and marker
- ▶ 5 toothbrushes
- ▶ 4 different whitening toothpastes
- ▶ Stopwatch
- ▶ Water

EXPERIMENTAL PROCEDURE

1. First, stain your "teeth." Instead of teeth, you'll use the rough, unfinished side of ceramic tiles. Put all the ceramic tiles into the bowl.

2. Follow the instructions on the instant coffee package, making enough coffee to cover the ceramic tiles completely. Let the tiles sit for 24 hours, remove them, and let them dry for another 24 hours.

3. Using the masking tape and marker, label each of the toothbrushes with the name of one of the toothpastes. Be sure to use each toothbrush only with its matching toothpaste. One toothbrush will be used with just water. Label each of the ceramic tiles as well.

4. Place some toothpaste from the first tube on the first toothbrush. Use the same amount you would usually use to brush your teeth.

5. Start the stopwatch and brush the first tile for 2 minutes. Be sure to brush over the entire surface of the tile. Brush from side to side and in circles. After 2 minutes, rinse the toothpaste off the toothbrush and the tile.

6. Repeat steps 4 and 5, brushing the other tiles with the other toothpastes. On the last tile, just use water without toothpaste.

7. Order the tiles from darkest to lightest and record the order.

8. Let the tiles dry and repeat the process 13 more times, or until there is no more color change. (This simulates brushing twice a day for one week.)

CONCLUSION

Which toothpaste whitened the quickest? Which one whitened the whitest? Did just brushing with water have any effect on the coffee stains? Do you think ceramic tiles are a good way to represent teeth? Compare the ingredients on the different toothpastes. Do any use the same whitening agents?

TAKE A CLOSER LOOK

Coffee and tobacco are the number one culprits in staining teeth. Because people are willing to pay a lot of money to remove or prevent these stains, there are hundreds of products out there that claim to whiten teeth. Toothpaste is the easiest way to whiten teeth because everyone uses it (or should!). However, most toothpastes don't list their whitening agent in the active ingredients, so it's difficult for consumers to tell exactly what is providing the whitening power. The active ingredient in most whiteners is *carbamide peroxide*, which acts like bleach on your tooth enamel.

WHAT ELSE YOU CAN DO

Try other whitening products that are not toothpastes, such as strips, gels, and "home remedies" like baking powder. Stain your tiles with something besides coffee. If you still have some teeth you (or a sibling) lost, try the experiment with real teeth.

Candle in the Wind

If you put a candle in a draft, the wax will drip down one side. It's a neat effect, but does it shorten the life of the candle?

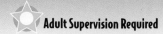
PROBLEM/PURPOSE

How does wind affect how fast a candle burns?

SAFETY: *Be sure to burn your candles in an area clear of curtains, paper, or other flammable materials. Do not leave burning candles unattended. Always have an adult present when dealing with an open flame. Don't wear loose clothing. If you have long hair, tie it back.*

EXPERIMENT SUMMARY

You'll burn candles in a variety of airflows to see which burns the quickest.

WHAT YOU NEED

▸ **Masking tape**
▸ **Permanent marker**
▸ **13 identical new candles**
▸ **Scale**
▸ **Notebook and pencil**
▸ **Lighter or matches**
▸ **Ruler**
▸ **Timer or clock**
▸ **Fan**

EXPERIMENTAL PROCEDURE

1. Use the masking tape and marker to label the bottom of 12 candles "1" through "12." Weigh each of the 12 labeled candles on the scale. Record their weights. Measure the heights of the candles with the ruler and record them as well.

2. Place candles 1 through 3 in an open space where the air is very still. Light the candles and let them burn for 1 hour. Use a timer or clock to be exact.

3. Weigh and measure the candles again. Record the data. Average the change in weight and height for this group of candles.

4. Place the unlabeled candle in front of a fan. Light the candle. Place the fan as close to the candle as you can get without blowing it out. This distance will vary depending on the strength of your fan. Measure and record this distance. Replace the test candle with candles 4 through 6.

5. Light the three candles and let them burn in front of the fan for 1 hour. Then weigh and measure the candles. Record the data. Average the change in weight and height for this group of candles.

6. Double the distance between the fan and the candles. Then repeat step 5 with candles 7 through 9.

7. Double the distance between the fan and the candles again so that the fan will be twice as far from the candles as it was in step 6. Repeat step 5 with candles 10 through 12.

8. Calculate the average change in weight and the average change in height of the candles for each distance from the fan.

Note: *If you have a variable-speed fan you can change the setting on the fan instead of the distance of the candles. (Make sure you use new candles each time, though.)*

CONCLUSION

The first trial without the fan is the control group. Call this "wind speed 0." The group of candles burnt closest to the fan is "maximum wind speed." When you double the distance between the fan and the candle, the wind speed is half the maximum speed. When you double the distance again, the wind speed is one-quarter the maximum speed. Make a graph of average candle height versus wind speed. Make a graph of average candle weight versus wind speed. Did the candles burn at different rates? Which changed more quickly, the weight or the height?

TAKE A CLOSER LOOK

Candles are one of the earliest sources of light. A candle is made of a wick, a clothlike string that is dipped in wax. When you light the wick, the heat melts the wax, which evaporates and turns into a gas. The gas burns instead of the wick, so the candle burns for much longer than the wick could. Wind blows the gas away before the flame can burn it, which makes candles in a drafty location burn more quickly.

WHAT ELSE YOU CAN DO

What is the effect of different types of wax on burn speed? Experiment with beeswax, paraffin, and gel candles. Does the room temperature affect burn time? Will candles burn more quickly in a warm room or a cold room? Test other factors you think might affect burn speed.

Soggy Popcorn

The search for the perfect bowl of popcorn means bigger, fluffier pieces of popcorn. How can you increase your chances of getting a perfect puff every time?

PROBLEM/PURPOSE

How does the amount of moisture affect the size and volume of popped corn?

EXPERIMENT SUMMARY

You'll store popcorn kernels at different moisture levels and then measure the size and volume of the corn after it's popped.

WHAT YOU NEED

▶ **Measuring cups**
▶ **3 cups (.7 l) of yellow popcorn kernels**
▶ **2 glass jars with lids**
▶ **Masking tape**
▶ **Marker**
▶ **Water**
▶ **Paper towel**
▶ **Hot air popper**
▶ **Large bowl**
▶ **Ruler**

EXPERIMENTAL PROCEDURE

1. Put 1 cup (275.5 ml) of popcorn into each of the jars. Use the masking tape and marker to label the jars "Sample A" and "Sample B."

2. Close the lid tightly on sample A.

3. Add ⅛ (34.4 ml) cup of water to sample B and close the lid tightly.

4. Put 1 cup (275.5 ml) of popcorn on the paper towel. Spread the kernels around evenly. Label the towel "Sample C."

5. Leave all samples in a cool, dry place for 7 days. Turn the glass jars over once a day. Record any visible changes to the kernels.

6. Preheat the air popper 1 minute before adding the first sample of popcorn. (You want the popper to be warm before beginning each trial.)

7. Pour ½ cup (137.8 ml) of sample A into the popper. Catch the popcorn in the large bowl.

8. With the ruler, measure 10 popped kernels and record their sizes. Calculate the average size. Rate the average size of all the popped kernels as follows:
large (more than ¾ inch [1.9 cm]),
medium (½ to ¾ inch [1.3 to 1.9 cm]),
small (less than ½ inch [1.3 cm]).

9. Pour the popped kernels into the measuring cup. Measure and record how many cups of popped corn were produced.

10. Repeat steps 6 through 9 with the remaining ½ cup (137.8 ml) of sample A kernels.

11. Repeat steps 6 through 10 for samples B and C.

CONCLUSION

Is there a difference in look and texture between the popped samples? Which sample popped the lowest volume? Which sample popped the highest volume? What about the biggest and smallest popcorn? How does the moisture level of the kernels affect popping volume, size, and texture of popped corn?

TAKE A CLOSER LOOK

Popcorn is made up of hard starch, a carbohydrate that stores energy, and a little bit of moisture. This moisture is locked inside the kernel's hard shell. As the cooking temperature rises to about 450°F (232.2°C), the moisture turns to steam and pressure begins to build. This continues until the shell cannot withstand the force any longer, and finally it POPS! The starch turns into the puffy white part of the popcorn.

There are a few reasons why popcorn may not pop as it should. Popcorn kernels tend to lose moisture as they age. To make sure your popcorn has the right amount of moisture, never store popcorn kernels in a refrigerator or freezer. This can dry them out very quickly. To maintain the ideal moisture content of about 13 percent, store popcorn at room temperature in a tightly covered glass jar.

WHAT ELSE YOU CAN DO

How do yellow popcorn kernels compare to white popcorn kernels? How does the color of the unpopped kernel affect the color after popping? Test the effects of refrigeration and freezing on kernels. How does it pop when exposed to the various conditions?

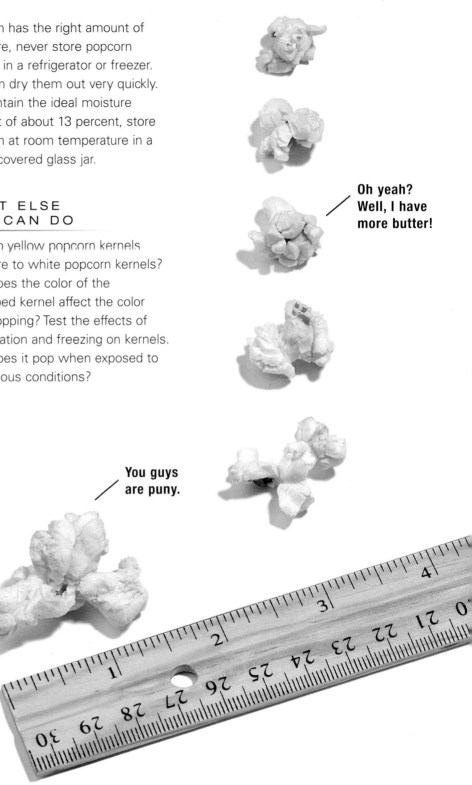

Oh yeah? Well, I have more butter!

You guys are puny.

Glossary

A

Abstract. The part of your project report that gives an overview of your experiment.

Accuracy. Measurements that are close to the true or real value.

Affect. A verb that means "to influence."

Air pressure. The force of air molecules against an object.

Apparatus. A piece of equipment, tool, or instrument that you use to perform your experiment.

B

Bernoulli's Principle. Fast moving air has a lower pressure than slow moving air.

Biological clock. An internal system that controls the timing of activities.

Biosphere. A self-sustaining environment.

C

Carbonation. The process in which a gas is added to a drink.

Center of gravity. The center of your body's mass.

Chemiluminescence. A chemical reaction which produces light.

Circadian rhythm. A biological clock that runs on a 24-hour day.

Cochlea. The part of your inner ear that lets you hear.

Coefficient of friction. A number that describes the friction between two surfaces.

Conclusion. The answer to your question.

Conduction. The transfer of energy through a substance.

Conductors. Materials that allow electrical charges to flow through them.

Controls. Things that stay the same throughout your experiment.

Cupola. The part of your inner ear that senses the motion of fluid and keeps you balanced.

D

Data. The measurements you take.

Density. The amount of stuff in a certain amount of space.

Dependent variable. The thing that changes as a result of changes to the independent variable.

E

Effect. A noun that means "consequence" or "result."

Electrical current. The flow of electrons from a positive terminal to a negative terminal.

Endothermic reaction. A chemical reaction that draws heat, cooling the substance.

Ethylene. The molecule released by ripening fruit.

Exothermic reaction. A chemical reaction that creates heat.

F

Filament. The part of lightbulb that glows when electricity heats it.

Friction. The force that occurs when two surfaces slide across each other.

H

Hydrophilic. Drawn to water.

Hydrophobic. Repelled by water.

Hypothesis. An educated guess at the answer to your question.

I

Impulse. A combination of force and the time the force is felt.

Independent variable. The thing you change in the experiment.

Insulators. Materials that do not allow electrical charges to flow through them.

Ionize. When a molecule splits into two or more charged atoms.

L

Lab notebook. Where you write down everything important about your experiment.

M

Magnetic force. A field created by moving electrons.

Molecule. A group of atoms attached together by a chemical force.

N

Nominal data. When your measurements are names or things rather than numbers.

O

Ordinal data. When your measurements are numbers.

Outliers. Weird data points that don't fit in with the rest of your measurements.

P

Pheromones. Chemicals that insects and animals use to communicate.

Photic organ. The part of a firefly that produces light.

Polar molecule. A molecule that is negatively charged at one end and positively charged at the other.

Precision. Measurements that are close to each other.

Prediction. What you think might happen in your experiment.

Procedure. The method you follow to answer your question.

Q

Qualitative value. Anything that can't be measured, such as color, texture, or month.

Quantitative value. Anything that can be measured.

R

Random error. When factors out of your control cause different measurements.

Refraction. The bending of light as it moves between two substances of different density.

S

Sampling. Collecting lots of data to ensure a minimal number of errors.

Scientific method. A set of guidelines scientists use to help them answer questions.

Selective Attention Theory. Naming colors requires more attention than reading words.

Semicircular canals. The part of your inner ear that detects how your head moves.

Speed of Processing Theory: Words are read faster than colors are named.

Standing wave. A vibration that fits within the length of the object vibrating, so that it appears to be still.

Stratosphere. The layer of the Earth's atmosphere that lies on top of the troposphere.

The Stroop Effect. The confusion of your brain when it receives two different forms of information.

Subject. Either the topic of your project or the people, animals, or things you're experimenting on.

Supersonic. When something travels faster than the speed of sound.

Systematic error. An error caused by doing the same thing wrong every time.

T

Terminal velocity. The point at which air resistance prevents a falling object from accelerating.

Thixotropic. A liquid that acts like a solid when it has been sitting undisturbed.

Topic. What your science fair project is about.

Trial. Repeating part of an experiment the same way you did before.

Troposphere. The layer of the Earth's atmosphere closest to the surface.

U

Umami. Savory flavor detected by taste buds.

V

Variable. The values that you're working with in your experiment.

W

Wavelength. The length between two peaks or two troughs in a wave.

Acknowledgments

Thanks to all of the people who made this book possible, especially:

Geoff and Sam Harris for their support and for accommodating experiments in the kitchen

Gina Barrier for her help with Science Fair Safety

Brent Smith for use of his science fair project in Fizzability

Participants in North Carolina's local, regional, and state science fairs for their hard work and inspiring projects

Rain Newcomb for her patience and editorial help

Thom Gaines for his excellent art direction and the photos on pages 33 and 50

The fantastic kids who modeled in this book:

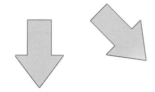

Rabb Scott

Anna

Sierra

Ingrid

Henry

Lillian

Marcus

Humpty Jr.

Bailey

Eva

Forrest

Index